FAMILY FUN NIGHT

BY DEANNA VAN DE BRAKE

A Write Fuzzy Book
Long Beach, CA USA

Family Fun Night
by DeAnna Van De Brake

Write Fuzzy Publishing ©2010.
1st printing.
Printed in USA

Family Fun Night Copyright 2010.
All Rights Reserved.

All Scripture from *New King James Version* of the Bible
Copyright © 1982 by Thomas Nelson, Inc. Used by permission. All rights reserved.

Published by Write Fuzzy Publishing.

Printed in Long Beach, CA USA.

No part of this book may be used or performed without written consent from the author, if living, except for critical articles or reviews.

Cover Designed by Joshua Grieve
Interior Layout by Lea C. Deschenes
illustrated by the Van De Brake Family
Edited by Nancy Counts and Derrick Brown
Proofread by Jennifer Roach
Type set in Helvetica Neue and Bell MT

To contact the author or company, send an email to brown@brownpoetry.com.

WRITE FUZZY PUBLISHING
LONG BEACH, CA

FAMILY FUN NIGHT

ABOUT THE BOOK 13

Lesson 1. THE BEGINNING
Genesis 1:1 15

Lesson 2. ADAM AND EVE
Genesis 2:18-20 17

Lesson 3. THE GARDEN OF EDEN
Genesis 3:8 18

Lesson 4. NOAH'S ARK
Genesis 6:18&19 19

Lesson 5. TOWER OF BABEL
Genesis 11:4-9 21

Lesson 6. ABRAHAM AND A NEW LAND
Genesis 13: 10-12 23

Lesson 7. THE PROMISE TO ABRAHAM
Genesis 18:10-14 25

Lesson 8. ISACC'S WIFE
Genesis 24:20 26

Lesson 9. ISAAC'S BLESSING
Genesis 27:24-27 28

Lesson 10. JACOB'S DREAM
Genesis 28:12 30

Lesson 11. JACOB AND ESAU MEET UP
Genesis 32:3 31

Lesson 12. JOSEPH'S DREAMS
Genesis 37:11 32

Lesson 13. THE DREAM
Genesis 39:21 33

Lesson 14. JOSEPH MEETS HIS FAMILY IN EGYPT
Genesis 44:4&5 35

Lesson 15. BABY MOSES
Exodus 2:10 37

Lesson 16. BURNING BUSH
Exodus 3:2, 4:1-4, 4:2&3 39

Lesson 17. THE PLAGUES
Exodus 7-11 41

Lesson 18. THE RED SEA
Exodus 14:14 &15 43

Lesson 19. MANNA, QUAIL AND WATER
Exodus 16:13 44

Lesson 20. THE TEN COMMANDMENTS
Exodus 20:3-17 45

Lesson 21. TWELVE SPIES
Numbers 13:1&2 48

Lesson 22. BALAAM & THE TALKING DONKEY
Numbers 22:28-30 50

Lesson 23. JERICHO
Joshua 6:3-5 51

Lesson 24. GIDEON
Judges 6:40 53

Lesson 25. SAMSON
Judges 13:5 55

Lesson 26. RUTH
Ruth 4:14&15 56

Lesson 27. HANNAH
1 Samuel 2:11 57

Lesson 28. SAMUEL
1 Samuel 3:10 58

Lesson 29. KING SAUL
1 Samuel 10:23, 24 59

Lesson 30. KING DAVID
1 Samuel 16:7 60

Lesson 31. DAVID AND GOLIATH
1 Samuel 17:23,24 61

Lesson 32. DAVID AND JONATHON
1 Samuel 20:4 63

Lesson 33. DAVID
Psalm 148:1-14 64

Lesson 34. SOLOMON
1 Kings 6:11-14 65

Lesson 35. ELIJAH AND THE RAVENS
1 Kings 17:4-6 67

Lesson 36. WIDOW'S OIL
1 Kings 17:12-14 69

Lesson 37. MOUNT CARMEL
1 Kings 18:37 71

Lesson 38. THE FLAMING CHARIOT
2 Kings 2:11 73

Lesson 39. JARS OF OIL
2 Kings 4:3-6 75

Lesson 40. THE SHUNEMMITE WOMAN
2 Kings 4:8 77

Lesson 41. NAMAAN
2 Kings 5:14 78

Lesson 42. JOSIAH
2 Kings 22:1&2 80

Lesson 43. DANIEL
Daniel 1:20 82

Lesson 44. SHADRACH, MESHACH & ABED-NEGO
Daniel 3:24&25 84

Lesson 45. DANIEL IN THE LION'S DEN
Daniel 6:16 86

Lesson 46. JONAH
Jonah 2:1,10 88

Lesson 47. MARY AND THE ANGEL
Luke 1:28-33 90

Lesson 48. JESUS'S BIRTH
Luke 2:4-7 92

Lesson 49. THE SHEPHERDS
Luke 2:8-12 94

Lesson 50. SIMEON AND ANNA
Luke 2:26-32, 36-38 95

Lesson 51. WISE MEN
Matthew 2:7-11 97

Lesson 52. WISE MEN ESCAPE
Matthew 2:12,16 99

Lesson 53. ZECHERIAH
Luke 1:13 101

Lesson 54. JESUS LOST
Luke 2:49 102

Lesson 55. JOHN THE BAPTIST
Matthew 3:13 103

Lesson 56. JESUS CALLS THE DISCIPLES
Luke 5:11 104

Lesson 57. WATER INTO WINE
John 2:11 105

Lesson 58. HOLE IN THE ROOF
Luke 5:23-24 106

Lesson 59. SERMON ON THE MOUNT
Matthew 6:34 108

Lesson 60. THE CENTURION
Luke 7:9 109

Lesson 61. PARABLE OF THE SEED
Matthew 13:18 111

Lesson 62. PARABLE OF THE MUSTARD SEED
Matthew 13:31,32 113

Lesson 63. GOOD FISH/BAD FISH
Matthew 13:47-51 115

Lesson 64. THE PEARL
Matthew 13:44-46 117

Lesson 65. WIND AND THE WAVES
Mark 4:41 119

Lesson 66. WOMAN HEALED
Mark 5:33 121

Lesson 67. JESUS FEEDS THE MULTITUDES
Matthew 14:19-21 123

Lesson 68. WALKING ON WATER
Matthew 14:22-33 124

Lesson 69. BLIND MAN
John 9:6&7 126

Lesson 70. THE TAX
Matthew 17:24-27 127

Lesson 71. THE GOOD SAMARITAN
Luke 10:36&37 129

Lesson 72. MARY AND MARTHA
Luke 10:38-42 131

Lesson 73. HEALING ON THE SABBATH
Luke 13:13 133

Lesson 74. THE PARABLE OF THE LOST SHEEP
Luke 15:7 134

Lesson 75. THE LOST COIN
Luke 15:8-10 136

Lesson 76. THE PRODIGAL SON
Luke 15:32 137

Lesson 77. THE TEN LEPERS
Luke 17:18&19 139

Lesson 78. JESUS AND THE CHILDREN
Psalm 127:3. Luke 18:15-17 141

Lesson 79. BLIND BARTIMAEUS
Luke 10:51&52 143

Lesson 80. ZACCHEUS
Luke 19:9 144

Lesson 81. THE WIDOW'S MITE
Mark 12:41-44 146

Lesson 82. THE POOL OF BETHESDA
Luke 5:8&9 148

Lesson 83. MARY ANOINTS THE FEET OF JESUS WITH PERFUME
John 12:3 150

Lesson 84. THE TRIUMPHAL ENTRY
John 12:12-15 151

Lesson 85. WASHING FEET
John 13:15 153

Lesson 86. THE LAST SUPPER
Matthew 26:26-28 154

Lesson 87. THE CRUCIFIXION
John 19:17&18 156

Lesson 88. RESURRECTION
Matthew 28:5&6 158

Lesson 89. JESUS AND THE FISH
John 21:7 161

Lesson 90. ASCENSION
Acts 1:9 163

Lesson 91. PENTECOST & FRUIT OF THE SPIRIT
Acts 2:1,2 & Galatians 5:22&23 165

Lesson 92. THE BEGGAR
Acts 9:3-5 168

Lesson 93. SAUL
Acts 9:1-19 170

Lesson 94. PAUL AND SILAS
Acts 16:25&26 172

Lesson 95. HEAVEN
Revelation 21:2 174

QUICK REFERENCE LESSON GUIDE 177

ABOUT THE AUTHOR 179

ABOUT THE BOOK

Family Fun Night is a bible based activity adventure for any sized family or children's ministry. As a Mom, I value the time our family gets to spend away from the television and busyness of life, to focus on our Creator and each other. This book is a collection of simple but thoughtful activities and games that color and bring to life some of our family's favorite Bible adventures. This collection started as a desire to introduce my young children to my very fun and amazing God, the God of the Bible. So we used a children's Bible for the pictures and these fun activities to make a big impression on them. I can not tell you how it warmed my heart when my children would beg for the next "family fun night". It was sometimes messy, sometimes crazy, but always fun! Raising a family can be busy, hectic, and sometimes stressful. God used this time not only to share and teach about the Lord and His word, but God helped us spend a moment to enjoy our children. The value of this quality time is truly an amazing gift we are blessed to share. Make a mess and have some fun!

LESSON 1. THE BEGINNING
Genesis 1:1

ACTIVITY:
Have each child make a play dough creation of something that God created.

SUPPLIES:
- Homemade play dough

    Recipe:
    - 2 cups flour
    - 1 cup of salt
    - 2 tbsp cream of tartar
    - 2 tbsp of oil
    - Food coloring, cinnamon or peppermint extract for fragrance

    Mix dry and liquid ingredients separately.

    Now mix both dry and liquid ingredients together.

    Heat slowly in a skillet until dough pulls together and away from the edge of pan.

    Add food coloring or flavor extract for scent (optional).

    Knead the dough.

    Store in a zip-lock bag until ready to use.

DISCUSSION:
God is the creator and all things come from Him.

REVIEW VERSE:
Genesis 1:1

1 In the beginning God created the heavens and the earth.

SUMMARY:
God is creator and created all we see, especially us. This is a powerful truth. We are not random accidents without any purpose. God designed us. We are unique. He gave us gifts, talents, personality traits no one else has. And out of all the things God created, we are His favorite. Tell your children the truth all the time "They are God's favorite out of all that he made."

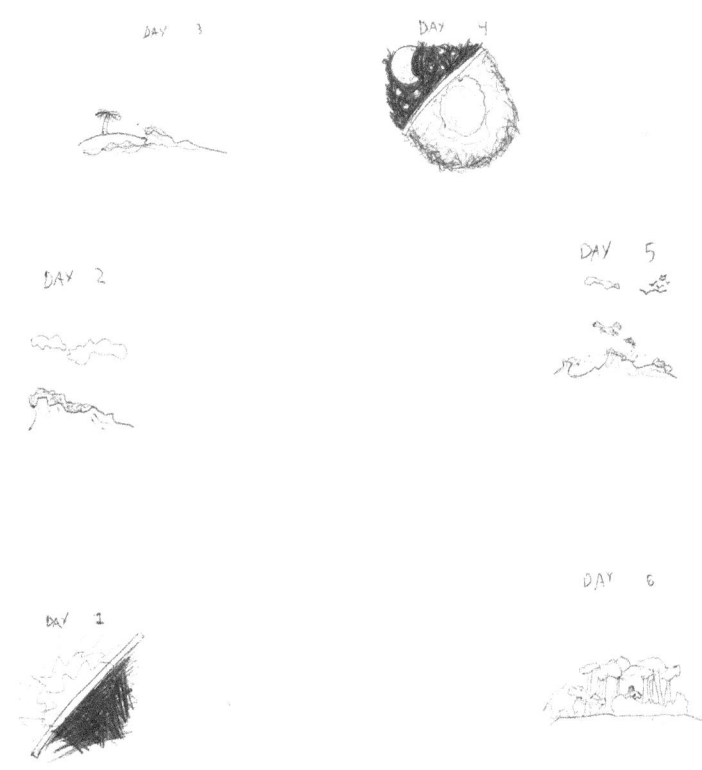

LESSON 2. ADAM AND EVE
Genesis 2:18-20

ACTIVITY:
Have the kids pretend to be Adam, naming the animals and sounds of the animals. Set up the animals all around the house. Pretend you're on a safari, zoo, jungle, or farm.

SUPPLIES:
- Stuffed animals (all you can find).

DISCUSSION:
Talk about how fun the animals are. Discuss the importance of friendship and how special marriage can be, and how it would be no fun to only have the animals to hang out with.

REVIEW VERSE:
Genesis 2:18-20

> *19 out of the ground the lord God formed every beast of the field and every bird of the air and brought them to Adam to see what he would call them. And whatever Adam called each living creature that was its name.*

SUMMARY:
Adam named all the animals. Can you imagine how long this took? When Eve was made, Adam finally had someone he could relate to.

LESSON 3. THE GARDEN OF EDEN
Genesis 3:8

ACTIVITY:

Play hide and seek.

The Seeker is like God looking for us, saying "Adam, Adam, where are you," or "Eve, Eve, where are you?" The person hiding is like Adam or Eve. The person trying to find them is like God trying to find us.

SUPPLIES:
- Just yourselves.

DISCUSSION:

God is always pursuing us because he wants a close relationship with us.

REVIEW VERSE:

Genesis 3:8

> *8 And they heard the sound of the LORD God walking in the garden in the cool of the day, and Adam and his wife hid themselves from the presence of the LORD God among the trees of the garden.*

SUMMARY:

This is a big event in history. Adam and Eve sinned by disobeying God. Sin and death entered the perfect world God made. Every person born will be born with a sinful nature. This means humans will naturally go against God. Later on in history, we will discover how God made a way for us to live forever with Him and be forgiven of going against God.

LESSON 4. NOAH'S ARK
Genesis 6:18&19

ACTIVITY:
Make your own ark just like Noah, but out of paper.

SUPPLIES:
- Paper
- Scissors
- Crayons
- Cotton Swabs
- Cotton Balls
- Lemon Juice
- Blue & Brown Construction Paper
- Animal Stickers

1. Get a piece of brown construction paper and cut it out like a boat.
2. Get a piece of blue construction paper and paste the boat onto it.
3. Optional (Glue cotton balls for clouds in the sky)
4. Here is a neat way to make raindrops:
5. Get a plastic bowl and cotton swabs (not cotton balls)
6. Fill the bowl with lemon juice
7. Using the cotton swab as a paintbrush, dab the swab into the lemon juice.
8. Put dots of lemon juice all over the blue construction paper to make the raindrops
9. The acid in the lemon juice will "bleach" the paper to make it look like it is raining.
10. It would be fun if you have any animal stickers to stick the animals on the boat
11. Title your masterpiece "Noah's Ark"

ACTIVITY #2:
Draw or make a rainbow and place over "Noah's Ark."

ACTIVITY #3:
Get an ice chest and place it in the bathtub or pool, have them grab some stuffed animals and pretend to be Noah in the ark. You could do this in a wagon and go for a "wild" bumpy off road ride.

DISCUSSION:
Talk about why the flood came and why the animals were on the ark. Discuss the colors in a rainbow and what the rainbow means about God always keeping His promises.

REVIEW VERSES:
Genesis 6:18&19

> *18 But I will establish My covenant with you; and you shall go into the ark—you, your sons, your wife, and your sons' wives with you. 19 And of every living thing of all flesh you shall bring two of every sort into the ark, to keep them alive with you; they shall be male and female.*

SUMMARY:
God wiped out every person alive at that time with a flood except for Noah and his family and those animals mentioned in the Bible. It rained for forty days and forty nights. God sent a rainbow as a promise that He would never destroy the earth with a flood. Even though God does bring righteous and just judgment, He was and is long suffering. If you read this portion of scripture you will see that God values human life. His heart hurt at how unkind and violent everyone was treating each other.

LESSON 5. TOWER OF BABEL
Genesis 11:4-9

ACTIVITY:
Who can build the biggest tower without it falling down?

SUPPLIES:
- Legos
- Blocks or dominoes

DISCUSSION:
Remember God is the best and even the things we can build, make, or think of is because God has made us able to do a lot of things! What are some other things we can build?

REVIEW VERSE:
Genesis 11:4-9

> *5 But the Lord came down to see the city and the tower .... 9Therefore its name is called Babel, because there the Lord confused the language of all the earth; and from there the lord scattered them abroad over all the earth.*

SUMMARY:
One of the oldest structures on earth is a ziggurat built by the Sumerians in the Middle East. The tower of Babel was probably a ziggurat. The people came together to build a name for themselves. Before this time everyone spoke the same language. God confused their speech and scattered them all over the earth. This is a good reminder that our purpose in life should be to proclaim the great name of God, not ourselves.

LESSON 6. ABRAHAM AND A NEW LAND
Genesis 13: 10-12

ACTIVITY:

1. Set out a treat in which it is obvious there is a pile of more crackers or a larger piece of pie.

2. Explain that it is good to let others go first and let others have the best or the most

3. Tell the kids they will be rewarded for letting mom or dad go first

4. Parents then pick the best and most for themselves

5. All sit down and eat

6. Afterwards, reward each child with twice as much as they had before

7. Explain God sees everything and rewards us, sometimes with stuff we can see and other times with stuff we can't see like joy and peace and favor.

SUPPLIES:
- Cookies, crackers, ice cream, candy, popcorn, or whatever snacks your kids enjoy.

DISCUSSION:
Abraham did not have to pick the best, be selfish, or greedy. Abraham was blessed by God far more than Lot was, even though at first, it seemed like Abraham was getting ripped off. Put others first, and in time you will see God blessing YOU!

REVIEW VERSE:
Genesis 13:10-12

> *And Lot lifted his eyes and saw all the plain of Jordan and that it was well watered everywhere (before the Lord destroyed Sodom and Gomorrah) like the garden of the Lord, like the land of Egypt as you go toward Zoar. Then Lot chose for himself all the plain of Jordan. And they separated from each other. 12 Abram dwelt in the land of Canaan...*

SUMMARY:
Abram was considered a nomad, or a wanderer. He had no land of his own until this point. God had blessed him so abundantly with livestock that there was a lot of confusion and strife between Lot's (his nephew) servants and Abram's. Abram let Lot choose first, and Lot choose the best of the two regions. Abram settled in Canaan. Yet God prospered Abraham so much people from other regions considered him a prince.

LESSON 7. THE PROMISE TO ABRAHAM
Genesis 18:10-14

ACTIVITY:

1. Write encouraging words on a small piece of paper, you can use verses or just say "I love you," "You are terrific," etc.
2. Fold up as small as possible in order to fit inside the balloon. Put the message inside the balloon and blow up the balloon.
3. Give one balloon to each child.
4. In order for the kids to find out what their blessing is, they have to pop their balloon.

SUPPLIES:

- Balloons
- Paper
- Pen, pencil, or marker

DISCUSSION:
God loves to bless us. What are some of the ways God does bless us? What does "bless" mean?

REVIEW VERSES:
Genesis 18:10-14

> *And He said, "I will certainly return......14 Is anything too hard for the lord? At the appointed time I will...and Sarah shall have a son."*

SUMMARY:
God promised Abraham He would be a father of many nations. He had no child with his wife Sarah at this point. After they were quite old, God brought some visitors to tell Abraham he would have a child next year at that time. Sarah laughed thinking that would be impossible at her age. God did exactly as He promised and Sarah had a son and they named Him Isaac which meant laughter.

LESSON 8. ISACC'S WIFE
Genesis 24:20

ACTIVITY:
Choose someone to be Rebekah. The others pretend to be camels (right hand and right foot or knee move up at the same time, then left hand and left foot move at the same time. "Rebekah" puts water in a bowl for each of the camels. "Camels" drink the water.

SUPPLIES:
- Bowl
- Water

DISCUSSION:
God smiles when we give with a good attitude and when we give more than what is asked for!

REVIEW VERSES:
Genesis 24:20

> *Then she quickly emptied her pitcher into the trough, ran back to the well to draw water, and drew for all the camels.*

SUMMARY:
The servant of Abraham wanted to find just the right person for his master's son to marry. He prayed to the Lord so He would know who to choose. He asked that the perfect person would offer a drink for himself as well as his camels. She did just that. He had 10 camels. She did it quickly, which was probably revealing of her heart. She was a giving servant, beautiful inside and out. Her name was Rebekah.

LESSON 9. ISAAC'S BLESSING
Genesis 27:24-27

ACTIVITY:
Make the treat first for the parent who will give the blessing.

The parent then extends their arms then gives a special blessing for each child. A blessing is kind words ("I love you", "You're the best.", "I am proud of you"), or telling your child about the gifts or talents you see in them and how God can use that for His glory (You are a great sharer, God can use this gift to make others feel special), or a special Bible verse to read to them.

You can use a verse for each child (Psalm 139, Is. 29:11).

Everyone eats the dessert and celebrates having received the special blessing.

SUPPLIES:
- Popcorn or favorite dessert of parent

DISCUSSION:
When we read God's word we hear how God wants to bless us and all the cool things he wants to say to us and about us.

REVIEW VERSES:
Genesis 27:24-27

> *Then he said, "Are you really my son Easu?"...27And he came near and kissed him; and he smelled...like the smell of a field which the Lord has blessed.*

SUMMARY:
Isaac and Rebekah had twin sons names Esau and Jacob. Since Isaac was old and could not see well, Jacob deceived his father and received the blessing that was reserved for the first born. The verbal blessing was very valuable in those days. Speaking kind words of approval as a parent can be just as important today in affecting the future success of your children. So don't be shy, tell them "They ROCK!" "They are the greatest kids in the whole wide world"!

LESSON 10. JACOB'S DREAM
Genesis 28:12

ACTIVITY:
Look around for rocks larger than a quarter. Decorate them by using paint or even permanent markers with adult supervision.

SUPPLIES:
- Rock and paint

DISCUSSION:
Have each child share/talk about something special God has done for them. The rock is made to help you remember God's goodness to you!

REVIEW VERSE:
Genesis 28:12

> *12 Then he dreamed, and behold, a ladder was set up on the earth, and its top reached to heaven; and there the angels of God were ascending and descending on it.*

SUMMARY:
As we learned in the previous chapter, Jacob was quite the deceiver. One night he dreamed of a ladder going to heaven. He also fell asleep on a hard rock and wrestled with the Lord. Jacob clung to him and begged to be blessed. Jacob's hip was touched by him. He walked away limping. His name was changed to Israel.

LESSON 11. JACOB AND ESAU MEET UP
Genesis 32:3

ACTIVITY:
Give presents to each other. (Parents may participate, too.)

SUPPLIES:
- Wrapping paper
- A small gift for each person

DISCUSSION:
When we hurt someone we should think of ways like Jacob did to make that person feel special again.

REVIEW VERSE:
Genesis 32:3

> *Then Jacob sent messengers before him to Esau his brother in the land of Seir, the country of Edom*

SUMMARY:
Jacob has an obvious change. He wants to bless his brother rather than take advantage of him. So he sends a servant ahead of him and many of his possessions as well to greet Esau in hopes to make amends.

LESSON 12. JOSEPH'S DREAMS
Genesis 37:11

ACTIVITY:
Bring each child into the kitchen one at a time.

Tell them in the eye how special and wonderful they are and how much you love them.

Tell them because of that they get the "ice cream of many colors."

SUPPLIES:
- Multi-colored ice cream (rainbow sherbet, Neapolitan ice cream)

REVIEW VERSE:
Genesis 37:11

11 And his brothers envied him, but his father kept the matter in mind.

SUMMARY:
Jacob was also deceived by his father-in-law. He was madly in love with Rachel and agreed to work for 7 years for his father-in-law so he could marry her. His father in law gave Jacob Leah instead. Jacob did not realize it until the morning. He had to work another 7 years for Rachel. Since Leah was not loved, God gave her many children. But Rachel had none. She finally had Joseph. Joseph became Jacob's favorite. Joseph dreamed about how he was a star and all the other stars and moon and sun would bow down to him. This made his half brothers very jealous. Then when he received the coat of many colors, that made them even more upset. They did sell him into slavery and told the father he had died.

LESSON 13. THE DREAM
Genesis 39:21

ACTIVITY:
Tell the kids that they need to do something good (clean room, give siblings a hug).

While they are being kind, the parents lightheartedly pretend to be upset, grab them (tie their hands up loosely if you wish) and throw them into "prison."

Let them go free and celebrate with dessert.

SUPPLIES:
- Something that can serve as a jail, and a dessert

DISCUSSION:
Talk about how sometimes things are hard when we do what is right.

Keep doing what is right and you will see God being good to you, if you don't give up.

REVIEW VERSE:
Genesis 39:21

> *21 But the LORD was with Joseph and showed him mercy, and He gave him favor in the sight of the keeper of the prison.*

SUMMARY:
The story of Joseph is such a testimony of always doing what is right, because God does see and will always reward you for doing good even at first it seems like you are being punished. Joseph was a slave and earned favor and received status from Potiphar (An Egyptian ruler at that time). Potiphar's wife tried to get Joseph to break the 7th commandment in the Bible, and he ran away. She lied about it. Joseph was put into prison. He even earned favor while in prison.

The baker and cup bearer had dreams. Joseph interpreted them correctly, of course giving glory to God for this ability. He asked them to remember him, but they did not. At least not until, Potiphar had a dream. The dream was about fat cows being swallowed up by skinny cows. The baker remembered Joseph. Joseph interpreted the dream to mean that Egypt would have abundance then famine. They would gather and save during the time of prosperity to help during the famine years. Joseph became second in command.

LESSON 14. JOSEPH MEETS HIS FAMILY IN EGYPT
Genesis 44:4&5

ACTIVITY:
Reenact the story.

Give each person the ingredients to make a banana split. Give once child a bunch of bananas, another a tub of ice cream, a package of nuts, whipped cream, a jar of cherries, a container of syrup. They will donate a portion of what they have for the greater cause of making a banana split for all to share.

One person in charge of the bananas brings a banana to be shared.

Each person donates a handful or one of whatever you have given them to hold. Example: One person donates a handful of nuts, another donates a scoop of ice cream, or syrup, a cherry, or whipped cream.

After all the supplies have been donated and the banana split has been prepared, send the kids to their room.

Pretend seven years have gone by and they have no food.

You call them in to come back and ask for food.

They all can dig in to the banana split.

SUPPLIES:
- Ingredients to make a banana split

DISCUSSION:
If we are greedy and keep our stuff all to ourselves, we will pay the consequences of that (no friends, empty heart, being unhappy). If we give and share, we will be given to and shared with when we are in need.

REVIEW VERSES:
Genesis 44:4&5

4 And Joseph said to his brothers, "Please come near to me." So they came near. Then he said: "I am Joseph your brother, whom you sold into Egypt. 5 But now, do not therefore be grieved or angry with yourselves because you sold me here; for God sent me before you to preserve life.

SUMMARY:
While the famine occurred in Egypt, it had spread to Canaan were Joseph was from and where his family still lived. Joseph's brothers came to Egypt to get food. They did not know Joseph was second in command, nor did they recognize him. They demonstrated repentance for how they treated their brother as Joseph gave them the run-a-round before he gave them food. Joseph revealed himself to them. He forgave them. His father and his family moved to live in Egypt. If you read this in the Bible there are many similarities and amazing symbolism of Jesus Christ, who He is and what He has done for us.

LESSON 15. BABY MOSES
Exodus 2:10

ACTIVITY:
Take the kids for a ride in the water in a "boat" (an ice chest or anything else you can think of).

Take them for a ride with something to cover (hide) them

Then you or another child pretend they get discovered and "drawn out" of the water.

SUPPLIES:
- Tub or pool of water
- Large ice chest

DISCUSSION:
Ask them how it may have felt to be Moses.

REVIEW VERSES:

Exodus 2:10

> *10 When the child grew older, she took him to Pharaoh's daughter and he became her son. She named him Moses, [a] saying, "I drew him out of the water."*

SUMMARY:
The Israelites grew while living in Egypt. Remember Jacob's name was changed to Israel, so all his descendants became Israelites. The Pharaoh was not sympathetic towards them as Potiphar had been. He was oppressive and feared them because of their numbers.

The Pharaoh wanted all the Hebrew boys to be killed. The mother of one of the baby boys hid him in the reeds to keep him safe. Pharaoh's daughter is the one who found him. After the baby was weaned, he was raised like a prince.

LESSON 16. BURNING BUSH
Exodus 3:2, 4:1-4, 4:2&3

ACTIVITY:
"A magic trick"

Without the kids knowing, roll a fake snake tightly in newspaper.

Pretend to be Moses and throw the rod down so the snake comes out.

Quickly hide the newspaper behind your back

SUPPLIES:
- Fake snake
- Newspaper

DISCUSSION:
Talk about how awesome God is and that this was no magic trick—it really happened, and why.

REVIEW VERSES:
Exodus 3:2

> *2 And the Angel of the LORD appeared to him in a flame of fire from the midst of a bush. So he looked, and behold, the bush was burning with fire, but the bush was not consumed.*

Exodus 4:1-4

> *1 Then Moses....3 And He said, "Cast....fled from it.*

Exodus 4:2&3

> *So the LORD said to him, "What is that in your hand?"*
> *He said, "A rod."*
> *3 And He said, "Cast it on the ground." So he cast it on the ground, and it became a serpent; and Moses fled from it.*

SUMMARY:
Moses had fled (because of a crime) from a life of luxury to living in the wilderness as a shepherd. God spoke to him in a burning bush of fire that did not burn up. This is when God called Moses to lead His people, the Hebrews, to the land of Canaan where they would no longer be in slavery.

LESSON 17. THE PLAGUES
Exodus 7-11

ACTIVITY:
Pretend to have a plague. Use rolled-up balls of newspaper to represent the different plagues. Every time there is a plague, dump out the rolled-up newspaper and throw them at each other, making various animal sounds.

When the plague gets cleared up, the kids throw balls of newspaper into the bag only to be dumped out again for the next plague.

SUPPLIES:
Newspaper rolled into little balls

DISCUSSION:
God sent these plagues to show the Israelites and the Egyptians, and all who heard of these things, that there is no other god like the true and living God, The God of the Israelites, The God of heaven and earth (many of these plagues were making fun of specific gods that the Egyptians worshipped).

REVIEW VERSES:
- Waters become blood - Exodus 7:17-18
- Frogs - Exodus 8:1,2,12-14
- Lice – Exodus 8:16-18
- Flies – Exodus 8:21,30
- Livestock Diseased – Exodus 9:3,6,7
- Boils – Exodus 9:10
- Hail – Exodus 9:16-18, 25, 26
- Locusts - Exodus 10:12
- Darkness - Exodus 10:21-23
- Death of all first-born – Exodus 11:4-7

SUMMARY:
When Moses went to Pharaoh and said The Israelites would like to freely go to a mountain to worship the God of the Hebrews, Pharaoh refused. God warned Pharaoh that there would be plagues that would strike the land if Pharaoh hardened his heart. When the plagues struck, he would say "Yes, you may go" as long as the plague would go away. But he always changed his mind. The last plague would be the death of all the first born unless the blood of the lamb was on the doorpost of your home. If it was the angel of death would pass over this home. This is symbolic of Jesus, being our Passover lamb. His blood on the cross is the only thing that will forgive us our sins, if we apply what he did to the doorposts of our heart (let Jesus reign in our life), the second death will Passover us (the second death is eternity apart from God).

LESSON 18. THE RED SEA
Exodus 14:14 &15

ACTIVITY:
Play tag. The parents pretend to be the Egyptians chasing the Israelites. The kids are the Israelites running to safety, which is the "Red Sea". If the parent runs into the sea, they have to pretend to die.

SUPPLIES:
A pretend body of water—you can use a blanket, draw one with chalk on the sidewalk, shape ropes in a square or circle, etc.

DISCUSSION:
The Lord is our protector. Why is he our protector?
Name some ways He protects us.

REVIEW VERSES:
Exodus 14:14 &15

> *14 The LORD will fight for you, and you shall hold your peace."*
>
> *15 And the LORD said to Moses, "Why do you cry to Me? Tell the children of Israel to go forward. 16 But lift up your rod, and stretch out your hand over the sea and divide it. And the children of Israel shall go on dry ground through the midst of the sea.*

SUMMARY:
After the final plague Pharaoh and the Egyptians were ready to let them go. But once again as all these people started to walk to the Promise Land, Pharaoh hardened his heart again and decided to chase after them. This is such an amazing story of the power of God. He held them back with fire. You would think this would get their attention not to be on the opposing side of God. The Israelites came to the Red Sea. Moses raised his rod the sea split and they walked, not on marshy wet swamp land, but dry ground. The fire subsided and Pharaoh's army went after them and they drowned in the Red sea.

LESSON 19. MANNA, QUAIL AND WATER
Exodus 16:13

ACTIVITY:
Have the kids go outside and say, "I'm hungry."

Then have the popcorn come down from the sky by parent being on the roof or on other side of the fence.

Then have the parent or kid be the rock hiding under a blanket with a squirt gun.

The kids say, "I'm thirsty."

"Moses" hits the rock with the rolled-up newspaper. Then water squirts out so that they can get a drink.

SUPPLIES:
- Blanket
- Squirt gun or water bottle
- Popcorn
- Rolled-up newspaper

DISCUSSION:
God takes care of us. Identify some ways God takes care of us. Help them understand His provision.

REVIEW VERSES:
Exodus 16:13

> *13 So it was that quails came up at evening and covered the camp, and in the morning the dew lay all around the camp.*

SUMMARY:
When the children of Israel were on their way to Canaan, the promise land, God took care of them in miraculous ways. He gave them water from a rock as well as manna and quail from the sky.

LESSON 20. THE TEN COMMANDMENTS
Exodus 20:3-17

ACTIVITY:
Draw a large number (1-10) on each piece of paper

Each child gets one or two commandments, depending how many children there are (parents may participate). Draw a picture that helps them to remember that commandment.

EXAMPLE:
1. No other God's before me –
Draw the number 1- keep God first

2. No idols –
Draw pictures of things you may sometimes like more than God like TV or toys.

3. Do not use the Lord's name in vain –
Spell the word GOD or JESUS surrounded by beautiful designs or things to remind us to use His name with respect.

4. Remember the Sabbath day and keep it holy –
Draw a picture of church, Christian friends, things you do at church.

5. Honor your father and mother –
Draw mom and dad along with green grass because of the promise that goes along with this commandment (so that you may live long in the land the Lord is giving you).

6. Don't murder –
No blood and guts please –
Draw people, life, babies, the things we get to enjoy in this life.

7. Do not commit adultery –
Draw wedding stuff.

8. Do not steal –
Draw eyes and hearts. These are what cause us not to be happy with the things God has given us.

9. Do not bear false witness –
Draw lips, mouth, and tongue.

10. Do not covet –
Draw happy faces and stuff with anti signs around them reminding us to be happy with what we have.

SUPPLIES:
- Crayons or markers
- Ten sheets of paper

DISCUSSION:
Discuss the importance of each command. Put these all over the house. Talk about them while they are doing them and as things come up. While you're eating dinner or watching a commercial (thou shall not covet is a good one), maybe even put one in the car.

REVIEW VERSE:
Exodus 20: 3-17

> *3 "You shall have no other gods before Me. 4 You shall not make for yourself a carved image—any likeness of anything that is in heaven above, or that is in the earth beneath, or that is in the water under the earth; 5 you shall not bow down to them nor serve them. For I, the LORD your God, am a jealous God, visiting the iniquity of the fathers upon the children to the third and fourth generations of those who hate Me, 6 but showing mercy to thousands, to those who love Me and keep My commandments. 7 You shall not take the name of the LORD your God in vain, for the LORD will not hold him guiltless who takes His name in vain. 8 Remember the Sabbath day, to keep it holy. 9 Six days you shall labor and do all your work, 10 but the seventh day is the Sabbath of the LORD your God. In it you shall do no work: you, nor your son, nor your daughter, nor your male servant, nor your female*

servant, nor your cattle, nor your stranger who is within your gates. 11 For in six days the LORD made the heavens and the earth, the sea, and all that is in them, and rested the seventh day. Therefore the LORD blessed the Sabbath day and hallowed it. 12 Honor your father and your mother, that your days may be long upon the land which the LORD your God is giving you. 13 You shall not murder. 14 You shall not commit adultery.

15 You shall not steal. 16 You shall not bear false witness against your neighbor. 17 You shall not covet your neighbor's house; you shall not covet your neighbor's wife, nor his male servant, nor his female servant, nor his ox, nor his donkey, nor anything that is your neighbor's."

LESSON 21. TWELVE SPIES
Numbers 13:1&2

ACTIVITY:
Your family is going to spy!

They are going to sneak around and try to catch someone BEING GOOD

Stay WITH your kids

If your child is shy, when they catch someone being good, you can be the one who actually goes up to the person telling what they did that was kind and give them the sticker or treat

SUPPLIES:
- Stickers or treat

Go to the store, mall or your neighborhood

DISCUSSION:
It's easy to look at the bad but God says we are fearfully and wonderfully made. We should see things the way Jesus does, and like Joshua and Caleb did. This is just a way to help us be a blessing to others.

REVIEW VERSE:
Numbers 13:1&2

> *1 And the Lord spoke to Moses, saying, "Send men to spy out the land of Canaan, which I am giving to the children of Israel: from each tribe of their fathers you shall send a man, every one a leader among them."*

SUMMARY:
The children of Israel have arrived to the promise land. God is ready to give them the land. He sends 12 spies, one from each of the tribes of Israel, to bring back a report, whether it is all God said it would be or not. 10 of the spies basically tell everyone that the land is indeed terrific, but the people are too much for them to handle. Two of the spies, Joshua and Caleb, bring back a report that says, we can do this, we are stronger and can overcome all of them. The people choose to believe that they were unable to defeat them, and decided not to take possession of the land. This is unbelievable considering all they had witnessed God do for them: he parted the sea, defeated the Egyptian army, fed and gave them drink in the wilderness, and much more. God almost wiped them out, but Moses begged God not to. So He relented. The Lord told them that this particular generation would die in the wilderness, because of their rebellion. Only Joshua and Caleb would enter into the promise land. It's amazing, but they still went against God, and decided to conquer the promise land without God's blessing. So, of course, the rebels of Israel were defeated and destroyed.

LESSON 22. BALAAM & THE TALKING DONKEY
Numbers 22:28-30

ACTIVITY:
Act out the story of Balaam and talking donkey. The parent is the donkey. The kid gets to be Balaam. The kid is on the parent's back. The parent or "donkey" stops. The kid beats the donkey with the newspaper. Then the donkey speaks.

SUPPLIES:
- Rolled-up newspaper

DISCUSSION:
God is looking out for us, even the things we know nothing about.

REVIEW VERSE:
Numbers 22:28-30

> *Then the LORD opened the mouth of the donkey, and she said to Balaam, "What have I done to you, that you have struck me these three times?" 29 And Balaam said to the donkey, "Because you have abused me. I wish there were a sword in my hand, for now I would kill you!" 30 So the donkey said to Balaam, "Am I not your donkey on which you have ridden, ever since I became yours, to this day? Was I ever disposed to do this to you?" And he said, "No."*

SUMMARY:
This is such a wild event in the Bible. A donkey talking is pretty amazing. But here we have Balaam who is asked to curse the Hebrews, whom God has blessed. Quite frankly, I think they deserved to be cursed, especially considering their rebellion against God. But God protects them without them knowing about it. He sends an angel to block Balaam. Then when Balaam opens his mouth with the intent to curse, he can only bless them.

LESSON 23. JERICHO
Joshua 6:3-5

ACTIVITY:
Act out the story in the Bible verse. Build the wall with blocks.

Walk around it like the story says. Then yell, blow trumpets, and knock it down.

SUPPLIES:
- Blocks
- Horn

DISCUSSION:
God is a mighty warrior—awesome in power. We just need to obey Him.

REVIEW VERSE:
Joshua 6: 3-5

> *3 You shall march around the city, all you men of war; you shall go all around the city once. This you shall do six days. 4 And seven priests shall bear seven trumpets of rams' horns before the ark. But the seventh day you shall march around the city seven times, and the priests shall blow the trumpets. 5 It shall come to pass, when they make a long blast with the ram's horn, and when you hear the sound of the trumpet, that all the people shall shout with a great shout; then the wall of the city will fall down flat. And the people shall go up every man straight before him."*

SUMMARY:
Forty years has passed, the old generation has all died in the wilderness. God brings them to the promise land again, Canaan. God raises up Joshua, the good spy, to lead them to victory. They knock down this fortified city by marching around the wall.

They end the last day with trumpets and shouts. The walls just collapse. It is so good to do things God's way, even when it doesn't make sense. Hopefully we can learn from history that we get destroyed living against God and blessed living for Him.

LESSON 24. GIDEON
Judges 6:40

ACTIVITY:
Read the story of Gideon in the Summary below or in the Bible first to be better prepared to act out this story.

Act out the story of Gideon:

1. Get a strip of cotton and act out Gideon's fleece before God. Gideon puts a dry piece of cotton on the ground—God made the ground wet with dew all around it. Next Gideon put a dry piece of cotton on the ground, when he woke up the cotton was wet and the ground totally dry. This helped Gideon know it was God who was asking him to fight.

2. For the attack, let the parents be the enemies and the kids the Israelites.

3. The parents pretend to sleep.

4. The kids then wake up the parents through banging pots and pans together or blowing trumpets or horns.

5. The parents pretend to be startled (bumping into each other, knocking each other down, etc.)

SUPPLIES:
- Roll of cotton
- Pots and pans or various instruments to blow in

DISCUSSION:
God is faithful to show us the right thing to do, even when we are not sure.

REVIEW VERSE:
Judges 6:36-40

> *40 And God did so that night. It was dry on the fleece only, but there was dew on all the ground.*

SUMMARY:
God raised up judges to lead the Hebrews after they had settled in the land of Canaan. Gideon was one of those judges. God wanted to save them from the Mideanites who were about to attack them. Gideon wanted to make sure it was truly the Lord sending them to attack. So Gideon put out a fleece (piece of wool) and asked for the fleece to be dry, but the ground all wet from dew. God did just that. Then he asked for just the opposite to occur, dry ground but the fleeced drenched in dew. That happened as well. Then God calls the men to fight and reduces the army from 20,000 to 300. Then they defeat their enemies by smashing clay pots and blowing trumpets and confusing their enemies. This is obviously an act of God. They want to honor Gideon, but Gideon wants God to receive all the praise.

LESSON 25. SAMSON
Judges 13:5

ACTIVITY:
Act out the story of Samson. One person gets to be Samson; the other builds a tower. Tie up Samson with toilet paper. He then prays and gets to push the tower over and falls down with it

SUPPLIES:
- Blocks or cereal boxes and shoe boxes
- Toilet paper

DISCUSSION:
There are big consequences or problems we could avoid if we always love and obey God.

REVIEW VERSE:
Judges 13:5

> 5 "For behold, you shall conceive and bear a son. And no razor shall come upon his head, for the child shall be a Nazirite to God from the womb; and he shall begin to deliver Israel out of the hand of the Philistines."

SUMMARY:
Another judge God raised up was Samson. God commanded his parents not to let him eat any unclean thing (as God revealed to the Israelites earlier which foods were clean and unclean), no fermented drink, and he could not cut his hair. God gave Samson strength as long as these things were followed. He could defeated many Philistines attacking him at once. They feared him so asked Delilah, the girl he loved, to find out where he gets his strength or what his weakness is. She finally found out. They wound up cutting his hair. He was also tied to two pillars. He cried out to God to bring judgment on the Philistines one last time. God gave him strength to knock down the pillars he was tied to and destroyed about 3,000 Philistines that day.

LESSON 26. RUTH
Ruth 4:14&15

ACTIVITY:
Throw popcorn on the lawn and see who can glean the most.

SUPPLIES:
- Popcorn

DISCUSSION:
Ruth is a great example of a very hard-working person. God richly blessed her faithfulness.

REVIEW VERSE:
Ruth 4:14&15

> *14 Then the women said to Naomi, "Blessed be the LORD, who has not left you this day without a close relative; and may his name be famous in Israel! 15 And may he be to you a restorer of life and a nourisher of your old age; for your daughter-in-law, who loves you, who is better to you than seven sons, has borne him."*

SUMMARY:
The story of Ruth occurs during the period of time that Israel was ruled by judges. Ruth is the daughter-in-law of Naomi. Her husband and both of her sons die in battle. Naomi is planning to return to Judah after living in Moab. Ruth wants to stay with her. Ruth is a kind-hearted lady. She works hard taking leftovers from the fields of a man named Boaz. The law allowed poor people to do this without paying anything for the food. This man marries Ruth. He doesn't just marry her; he redeems her. This means, since he is the next willing, living relative he buys from Naomi all that used to be her husband's a long time ago, including Ruth. Any children Boaz and Ruth have will carry on the name of Ruth's previous husband.

LESSON 27. HANNAH
1 Samuel 2:11

ACTIVITY:
Make a Christmas/Birthday wish list. Have the kids go through a toy catalog and circle all they want, or write down what they want and draw pictures next to it. Mom and Dad can make their own list, too. Then go back and ask the important questions in the discussion.

SUPPLIES:
- Toy catalog if you have one, or paper and a pencil

DISCUSSION:
Why do we want the stuff?

How could we use it to do what Jesus would want?

What does Jesus want? (People to be saved, loved, forgiven.)

When we are asking for stuff, don't forget to say thank you for what we already have, what He has done, and thank you for who He is. It helps our heart stay happy and content.

REVIEW VERSE:
1 Samuel 2:11

> *11 Then Elkanah went to his house at Ramah. But the child ministered to the Lord before Eli the priest.*

SUMMARY:
Hannah wanted a child, but was unable to have one. She pleaded with God for a child and promised to devote him to the Lord. God granted her request. She named him Samuel. After he was weaned, Samuel lived with the priest, Eli, and served God all of his life at the place of worship.

LESSON 28. SAMUEL
1 Samuel 3:10

SUPPLIES:
- Wrap up something special.

ACTIVITY:
Act out the story of Samuel. Each kid takes turns pretending to be Samuel. Set up a tent with blankets around a table or use cushions to make a special sleeping place. Call the child by their name. Then they are to respond "Speak, Mom/Dad, your servant is listening." Whisper where the special something is located.

DISCUSSION:
It's great to be quiet to listen to God and have a heart to do what he wants us to do.

REVIEW VERSE:
1 Samuel 3:10

> *10 Now the LORD came and stood and called as at other times, "Samuel! Samuel!" And Samuel answered, "Speak, for Your servant hears."*

SUMMARY:
Samuel became a prophet of the Lord. He heard from the Lord as a young child. Kings sought Samuel out to hear what the Lord was saying to them. They did not always like what he had to say.

LESSON 29. KING SAUL
1 Samuel 10:23, 24

ACTIVITY:
Each child gets a turn to be a king or queen.

When it is their turn to be king or queen, they get picked up and cheered as loudly as possible. Say great blessings to them, like "Long live King/Queen (your child's name)."

SUPPLIES:
- Crown (tin foil with glitter works)

DISCUSSION:
Don't be like Saul and turn away from God, always love God the most!

REVIEW VERSE:
1 Samuel 10:23, 24

> *23 So they ran and brought him from there; and when he stood among the people, he was taller than any of the people from his shoulders upward. 24 And Samuel said to all the people, "Do you see him whom the LORD has chosen, that there is no one like him among all the people?" So all the people shouted and said "Long live the King."*

SUMMARY:
The story of Saul is a very heart breaking one. He starts off as this amazing young man. He is humble. He is respectful and generous. When he becomes King, unfortunately, he worships God for show only not from his heart. He is full of pride, and self. He wants all the praise for himself. He becomes insanely jealous of David because he is the new hero in town. David is completely loyal to King Saul, yet Saul wants to see him destroyed. Saul, sadly, shows no sign of repentance and ends up self-destructing. My dear sweet friend, are you living a life to please yourself or to please the Lord? You either serve money or God. If you are not living for Jesus, you will self-destruct. I encourage you to give your heart completely to following Him. You will be blessed beyond what you could ever imagine!

LESSON 30. KING DAVID
1 Samuel 16:7

ACTIVITY:
Make a backwards valentine card. Leave the outside plain. Decorate the inside.

SUPPLIES:
- Red, pink, or white construction paper or cardstock, pink or white
- Scissors
- Glue, glitter, lace, buttons, ribbons, or other miscellaneous craft items

DISCUSSION:
God is always looking at the beauty on the inside of us. If we look different on the outside, but we love Him and others, it is like a beautiful valentine card to Jesus.

REVIEW VERSE:
1 Samuel 16:7

> *7 But the LORD said to Samuel, "Do not look at his appearance or at his physical stature, because I have refused him. For the LORD does not see as man sees; for man looks at the outward appearance, but the LORD looks at the heart."*

SUMMARY:
David was just a shepherd boy, when God choose him as king. His father did not even think to consider him when Samuel asked Jesse, David's father, to bring all his sons out in order to anoint one of them as the future king. We will see that David sinned a lot, but his heart was truly broken when he blew it. He constantly turned to God to pour out his heart and gain strength, wisdom, help, comfort, forgiveness and much more. David relied on God. God called him a man after His own heart. How cool is that!

LESSON 31. DAVID AND GOLIATH
1 Samuel 17:23,24

ACTIVITY:
Act out the story of David and Goliath.

1. Have a child ride on Daddy's shoulders or stand on a chair.

2. Have a long robe covering Daddy so it just looks like a big man with a child's head.

3. Act out the story, taking turns to be David and Goliath.

SUPPLIES:
- Home-made slingshot, or rolled-up newspaper, or nerf balls for the stone

DISCUSSION:
Talk about how it felt to be taller than everyone else. What did God do for David?

REVIEW VERSE:
1 Samuel 17: 23, 24

> *23 Then as he talked with them, there was the champion, the Philistine of Gath, Goliath by name, coming up from the armies of the Philistines; and he spoke according to the same words. So David heard them. 24 And all the men of Israel, when they saw the man, fled from him and were dreadfully afraid.*

SUMMARY:
David was young and Goliath was huge. Goliath and the Philistines were threatening the Israelites. David asked who would go and fight Goliath. Everyone was scared. David knew the Lord had wanted to defeat these people who were against God and who wanted to take away the land God had given them as well as threaten their very lives.

David knew God was for the Israelites in this situation and would hand the Philistines over to the Israelites only if they were willing to make a stand and fight. David volunteered. He grabbed his sling shot and came to Goliath in the name of the Lord. He proclaimed that God would fight for him. He took one shot and the rock hit him between the eyes and he fell down dead. David became an instant hero among his people.

LESSON 32. DAVID AND JONATHON
1 Samuel 20:4

ACTIVITY:
Make a friendship bracelet. String the fruit loops on the string. Tie it when it's the appropriate length.

SUPPLIES:
- Fruit loops (or beads, if the child is old enough)
- String

DISCUSSION:
It is good to tell our friends how special they are, and to think of ways to help them and be kind to them.

REVIEW VERSE:
1 Samuel 20:4

4 So Jonathan said to David, "Whatever you yourself desire, I will do it for you."

SUMMARY:
After David slew Goliath, he came to live with the King Saul. During this time he became good friends with Saul's son Jonathan. Jonathan was a friend to David by betraying his own father who wanted to do away with David for no good reason, other than jealousy. David in turn showed kindness to Jonathan, when David became king he searched the land for anyone remaining from Jonathan's family and found Jonathan's son Mephibosheth who became crippled when his nurse fled for safety. David took him into his palace and treated him like a prince.

LESSON 33. DAVID
Psalm 148:1-14

ACTIVITY:
Go outside and shout awesome things about God. Talk about some of God's qualities. After this sing a praiseful worship song.

SUPPLIES:
Loud things like instruments.

DISCUSSION:
Telling God how awesome He is through praise and worship is the greatest thing we can ever do.

REVIEW VERSE:
Psalm 148:1-14

> *2 Praise Him all His angels;...14 And He has exalted the horn of his people...Praise the Lord*

SUMMARY:
David wrote many Songs and Poems to express his love for God, as well as many cries for help. He truly was a man after God's own heart.

LESSON 34. SOLOMON
1 Kings 6:11-14

ACTIVITY:
Build a temple with blocks.

SUPPLIES:
- Blocks

DISCUSSION:
Solomon went all out when he built this temple for the Lord. We should go all out when we do things for God like doing what our parents say—don't just pick up your room like they said, but get a little crazy and maybe put away your shoes too. You are doing it for Mom, Dad, and Jesus too! Give Him your best, not your worst (that would be an attitude, a sigh, rolled eyes).

Parents, don't forget that if you sigh when your kids ask you for something, they will too. Don't give the best to your outside ministry and leftovers to your family. At least smile the next time they ask you for something. What goes around comes around.

REVIEW VERSE:
1 Kings 6:11-14

> *11 Then the word of the LORD came to Solomon, saying: 12 "Concerning this temple which you are building, if you walk in My statutes, execute My judgments, keep all My commandments, and walk in them, then I will perform My word with you, which I spoke to your father David. 13 And I will dwell among the children of Israel, and will not forsake My people Israel." 14 So Solomon built the temple and finished it.*

SUMMARY:
David's son who became king was Solomon. God asked Solomon if he could have anything in the world what would he want. Solomon asked for wisdom. God said because he asked for this instead of riches, God would give him both. Solomon with all his wealth and peace from his enemies decided to build a temple for God instead of the tabernacle made of tents for a place of worship.

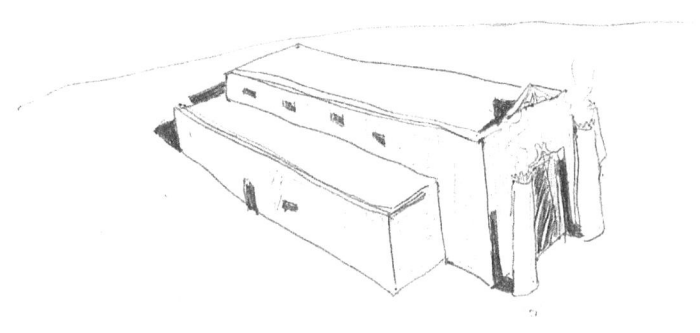

LESSON 35. ELIJAH AND THE RAVENS
1 Kings 17:4-6

ACTIVITY:
Act out the story of Elijah.

1. One person is Elijah.

2. They camp out by a source of water.

3. The food comes via the "ravens" (which is actually a paper airplane filled with popcorn).

4. Take turns.

SUPPLIES:
- Popcorn
- A source of water
- Paper
- Black construction paper
- Source of water (garden hose, bucket, spigot, sprinkler)

DISCUSSION:
God always takes care of us, sometimes in very unusual ways!

REVIEW VERSE:
I Kings 17:4-6

> *4 And it will be that you shall drink from the brook, and I have commanded the ravens to feed you there." 5 So he went and did according to the word of the LORD, for he went and stayed by the Brook Cherith, which flows into the Jordan. 6 The ravens brought him bread and meat in the morning, and bread and meat in the evening; and he drank from the brook.*

SUMMARY:
Elijah was a prophet during the reign of a very wicked King named Ahab and his even more wicked wife Jezebal. King Ahab encouraged the Israelites to worship Baal, a false god. He also had most all the prophets of the true and living God wiped out. Elijah was on the run for his life, but here is an example of how God took care of him.

LESSON 36. WIDOW'S OIL
1 Kings 17:12-14

ACTIVITY:
Make "doughnuts" out of refrigerated biscuits. Adult supervision and participation required.

1. Put 2 tbsp oil in a separate jar (enough to cover the skillet and pieces of dough.)

2. One person is the widow and gives all she has.

3. Make the doughnuts. Fill that jar up with 2 more tbsp of oil.

4. Put the oil in the skillet and let it heat up for a couple of minutes.

5. Divide the biscuits in quarters.

6. Put them in the oil.

7. Once they are cooked and slightly cool, roll them in sugar.

SUPPLIES:
- Refrigerated biscuits
- Oil
- Cinnamon sugar/powder sugar

DISCUSSION:
Explain how the widow's jar never ran out, even though she gave all she had. God fills us up with so much joy, that we can give and give and give and never run out!

REVIEW VERSE:
1 Kings 17:12-14

> *12 So she said, "As the LORD your God lives, I do not have bread, only a handful of flour in a bin, and a little oil in a jar; and see, I am*

gathering a couple of sticks that I may go in and prepare it for myself and my son, that we may eat it, and die." 13 And Elijah said to her, "Do not fear; go and do as you have said, but make me a small cake from it first, and bring it to me; and afterward make some for yourself and your son. 14 For thus says the LORD God of Israel: 'The bin of flour shall not be used up, nor shall the jar of oil run dry, until the day the LORD sends rain on the earth.'"

SUMMARY:
God told Elijah that a poor widow was the one He had selected to provide for him. He went to the widow's house and asked for some bread. She used the last of her oil to make him some bread, expecting to die. God promised the widow that as long as there was no rain, she would never run out of oil or flour. God is our provider. He sometimes chooses to provide for us in the out of the ordinary ways.

LESSON 37. MOUNT CARMEL
1 Kings 18:37

ACTIVITY:
Act out the story

1. Make an ox out of construction paper.
2. Put it in a pot as the false worshippers did.
3. Talk about how nothing happened.
4. Now Elijah did the same thing.
5. Cut the ox into pieces.
6. Pour tons of water in the pot and around the pot.
7. When He prayed, Fire came from heaven and burned up the sacrifice and everything on it, even the altar.
8. Throw the lighted match (parent supervision required) into the drenched pot. Explain how it is unusal for a fire to be so powerful that water does not make it go out. But God did something out of the ordinary that day, because the fire devoured the water instead of the water making the fire completely go out.

SUPPLIES:
- Matches
- Construction paper

DISCUSSION:
Talk about the true God and that there is only one God.

REVIEW VERSE:
1 Kings 18:37

> *37 Hear me, O LORD, hear me, that this people may know that You are the LORD God, and that You have turned their hearts back to You again.*

SUMMARY:
This account of Elijah confronting the false god, Baal, is awesome. God tells Elijah to go have a "competition" to see who the real GOD is. They are to ask their god to send fire from heaven to receive their offering. The Baal worshipers go first. They are there all day long. Elijah mocks them and encourages to shout louder to their god who might be sleeping. Absolutely nothing happens. When it is Elijah's turn, he puts water all over the altar. He asks God to send down fire from heaven so everyone knows who the real God is. The fire of God fell from heaven. It consumed not just the bull sacrifice, but the stones and wood dust and the water as well. Of course everyone can't help but proclaim that the Lord, He is God!

LESSON 38. THE FLAMING CHARIOT
2 Kings 2:11

ACTIVITY:
Go for a Flaming Chariot Piggy Back ride.

What to do:

Go outside.

Parents get on all fours or pull the child in a wagon. Parents light and hold candles or sparklers as they give their child a ride.

SUPPLIES:
- Sparklers or Candle

DISCUSSION:
It's a great thing to want God's power in your life. Pray for it and ask for the Holy Spirit to be like the flaming chariot in your heart, burning and always desiring more of Jesus.

REVIEW VERSE:
2 Kings 2:11

> 11 Then it happened, as they continued on and talked, that suddenly a chariot of fire appeared with horses of fire, and separated the two of them: and Elijah went up by a whirlwind into heaven

SUMMARY:
Elijah has an apprentice prophet named EliSHa. God sends down a flaming chariot and sweeps him to heaven. Elisha asks his mentor Elijah for a double portion of his spirit. Elijah said if he sees him swept away then God would answer his request. Elisha does indeed see Elijah taken to heaven by a flaming chariot.

LESSON 39. JARS OF OIL
2 Kings 4:3-6

ACTIVITY:

Ministry to a widow or the poor.

Do you know any widows or single parents
or children in a group home?

As a family pray about what God would want you to do for them.

Do it right after reading this story so the kids understand the
Bible is meant for us to apply to our hearts as we hear it.

Some ideas:

Pick flowers and put in a jar with a pretty bow and a thoughtful card.

Pick out some bubble bath and lotion at a local dollar store.

Go to the grocery store and have each child pick one non-perishable
food item and deliver it to the family you know or a local church.

SUPPLIES:
- None.

DISCUSSION:

God helps the widow and the poor. It makes Jesus smile when we do.
Not only that, we will be rewarded in heaven for helping others.

REVIEW VERSE:
2 Kings 4:3-6

3 Then he said, "Go, borrow vessels from everywhere, from all your neighbors—empty vessels; do not gather just a few. 4 And when you have come in, you shall shut the door behind you and your sons; then pour it into all those vessels, and set aside the full ones."

5 So she went from him and shut the door behind her and her sons, who brought the vessels to her; and she poured it out. 6 Now it came to pass, when the vessels were full, that she said to her son, "Bring me another vessel."

And he said to her, "There is not another vessel." So the oil ceased.

SUMMARY:
Elisha meets up with a widow who is about to have her sons taken away from her to pay her creditors. Elisha has them bring empty jars. They pour oil from one to another until there are no more jars. They sell it to pay off the debt and live on the rest.

LESSON 40. THE SHUNEMMITE WOMAN
2 Kings 4:8

ACTIVITY:
Have dinner or dessert in a high place, like a bunk bed or roof. (Be careful!)

SUPPLIES:
- Dinner or dessert
- A high place like a bunk bed or roof

DISCUSSION:
Pray for other people. Discuss the importance of prayer.

REVIEW VERSE:
2 Kings 4:8

> 8 One day Elisha went to Shunem. And a well-to-do woman was there, who urged him to stay for a meal. So whenever he came by, he stopped there to eat.

SUMMARY:
Here is another example of God taking care of Elisha's need through this hospitable lady. She opens her home for Elisha to stay.

LESSON 41. NAMAAN
2 Kings 5:14

ACTIVITY:
Put tape or stickers on a small stuffed animal and pretend it has leprosy. Dunk the stuffed animal in water so it can be "cleansed."

You can place tape or sticker dots on the child and if the weather is warm they can "dunk" in a small pool, or the tub.

SUPPLIES:
- Small stuffed animal
- Pieces of tape or sticker dots

DISCUSSION:
The Bible uses leprosy as a symbol of what sin is like. It spreads; there is no cure except when God miraculously touches us. Leprosy was so serious they would lose feeling in their hands and feet. If they got cut, hurt, or bitten, they would not feel it. Leprosy also caused them to be isolated and all alone. We need to be cleansed of the bad things we've done through what Jesus did for us on the cross and then daily by the washing that comes from reading the Word of God.

REVIEW VERSE:
2 Kings 5:14

> *14 So he went down and dipped seven times in the Jordan, according to the saying of the man of God; and his flesh was restored like the flesh of a little child, and he was clean.*

SUMMARY:
Namaan went to Elisha the prophet to see if he could pray for him to get healed of his disease called leprosy. Elisha told him to dip in the Jordan seven times and then he would be healed. Namaan did not want to do this. He expected God to use Elisha by waving his hand over him or at least dip in waters more desirable. His servants urged

him to do it. He did and was healed. Sometimes we expect God to answer our prayers the way we were hoping. We have to trust His kind heart and that He is smarter than we are, and follow His plan even when its different than our own.

LESSON 42. JOSIAH
2 Kings 22:1&2

ACTIVITY:
Build the temple with the blocks, then write on slips of paper what Jesus wants each of you to do (such as being kind, being thoughtful, etc.). Put the slips of paper in the "temple."

SUPPLIES:
Blocks and a crown

ACTIVITY #2:
Get a long rope and make a course with it. See if they can walk on the straight path of the rope without falling to the left or right. How fast can everyone do it? The path is doing things the way God wants us to. Falling off the path is doing things our own way.

DISCUSSION:
Try not to forget what God wants you to do. What are some things you can do to help you remember these this

REVIEW VERSE:
2 Kings 22:1&2

> *1Josiah was eight years old when he became king, and he reigned thirty-one years in Jerusalem. His mother's name was Jedidah, the daughter of Adaiah of Bozkath. 2And he did right in the eyes of the Lord, and walked in all the ways of his father David; he did not turn aside to the right hand or to the left.*

SUMMARY:
King Josiah was the youngest king in Judah's history. When the law was found and read to him, he tore his clothes. This was a symbol of grief and great anguish. All the sin he and his people were committing overwhelmed the king. He was on his face before God to ask for mercy and to give them a second chance to do what was right. God showed them mercy and King Josiah did what was right in the eyes of the Lord.

LESSON 43. DANIEL
Daniel 1:20

ACTIVITY:
Eat vegetables and have a contest of strength.

After you eat a vegetable, say:

1. Who can open the peanut butter jar? (Use that as dip for celery.)

2. Who can break this carrot in half?

3. See if the kids can do push-ups or do more push-ups than mom or dad

4. Have a race and the parents have a handicap (like a blindfold, tied feet, etc.)

SUPPLIES:
- Fresh vegetables

DISCUSSION:
It is important to rely on God for strength and wisdom because He knows what's best.

REVIEW VERSE:
Daniel 1:20

> *20 And in all matters of wisdom and understanding about which the king examined them, he found them ten times better than all the magicians and astrologers who were in all his realm.*

SUMMARY:
When Israel had turned their backs on God, God warned them. He told them they would become captives and no longer free if they did not repent of worshipping other gods as well as all the evil associated with that. They did not listen. The Chaldeans, who were

from Babylon attacked and conquered them. The king was King Nebuchadnezzar. Israel no longer had a king, but were now slaves. The king, however choose a few strong young men from Israel to serve in the kings courts and be taught the ways of the Chaldeans. Daniel, Shadrach, Meshach and Abednego were some of these young men. They refused to eat unclean food that God's law had told them not too. They did this with respect. They told their supervisors to test them out and see who was stronger, the ones who ate just vegetables or the ones who ate the king's food. After 10 days these young men looked stronger and better than all the rest. They looked so good the supervisors gave all the young men Daniel's food.

LESSON 44. SHADRACH, MESHACH & ABED-NEGO
Daniel 3:24&25

ACTIVITY:
Act out this story of Shadrach, Meshach, and Abed-Nego. Adult supervision required, please do this outdoors.

Have one parent pretend to be the King. The "King" says "You must bow down to me." The children in unison say "No way." The "King" puts the kids into a pretend "fiery furnace" (cardboard box, inside of four chairs enclosed to make a circle) The parent walks around the outside with sparklers or a candle to represent a fiery furnace.

When the "King" isn't looking, have a parent or another child enter the "furnace". When the "King" checks on them he sees that there are four instead of three. He lets them go free.

SUPPLIES:
- Sparklers for the "fire"

DISCUSSION:
Obey God even when it is not fun, then watch and see what HE does for YOU!

REVIEW VERSE:
Daniel 3:24&25

> *24 Then King Nebuchadnezzar was astonished; and he rose in haste and spoke, saying to his counselors, "Did we not cast three men bound into the midst of the fire?"*
>
> *They answered and said to the king, "True, O king."*
>
> *25 "Look!" he answered, "I see four men loose, walking in the midst of the fire; and they are not hurt, and the form of the fourth is like the Son of God."*

SUMMARY:
Shadrach, Meshach and Abednego refused to bow down to the golden statue. The king threatened to throw them into the fiery furnace. They still refused. The Lord protected them so much, they did not even smell like smoke when they exited the furnace. They also noticed a fourth man in the furnace was God's Angel.

LESSON 45. DANIEL IN THE LION'S DEN
Daniel 6:16

ACTIVITY:
Make masks and act out the story of Daniel in the lion's den.

Get a brown bag and cut out holes for the eyes.

For the mane, use precut strips of orange or yellow paper. Make strips 1 inch by about 3 inches. Roll the strips around a pencil to curl and glue them around the face of the mask. Act out the story: first, one parent is Daniel. The lions are nice and cuddle with him. Next, the bad guy (another parent) gets thrown in the den. Attack!

SUPPLIES:
- Brown paper bags
- Strips of orange or yellow paper
- Glue

DISCUSSION:
Discuss how to always live a life pleasing to God. Don't live to please man. Why?

* Don't forget Ephesians 6:1 Children obey your parents in the Lord- when we obey our parents, it pleases the Lord.

REVIEW VERSE:
Daniel 6:16

> *16 So the king gave the command, and they brought Daniel and cast him into the den of lions. But the king spoke, saying to Daniel, "Your God, whom you serve continually, He will deliver you."*

SUMMARY:
There is a new king, his name is Darius. He was a king of the Medes who overthrew the Chaldeans. The wise men who worked for the King were very jealous of Daniel and the favor he had with King Darius. They schemed to trap Daniel by telling the King that for thirty days no one should petition any god or man except the king. They knew Daniel prayed to God all the time. He indeed prayed as usual. The wise men threw Daniel into the lion's den, the king very sad by this, but had to uphold the law he had signed. When Daniel was alive the king was so happy. He threw the wise men and their families into the lion's den instead.

LESSON 46. JONAH
Jonah 2:1,10

ACTIVITY:
Prepare these sensory items before doing this activity.

Discover what it was like in the belly of the whale.

Set up a place to look like the inside of a fish. Make an area dark with blankets over a table, couch or bed.

Everyone uses their five senses:

Smell – Open the can of smelly tuna to get a good whiff.

Feel - Put your hands in the slime (Jell-O/nylons filled with oatmeal)

Taste – Give everyone a taste of salt, because everything was very salty.

Hear - Make rumbling and loud burping sounds if you can. (A sip of soda helps!)

Sight – Ketchup. It was very bloody and gross and rather dark.

How do you feel right about now? How do you think Jonah felt?

SUPPLIES:
- Something smelly, like tuna
- Salt
- Slime (prepared Jell-O, or mix borax with glue and water)
- Old nylons stuffed with wet oatmeal for intestines
- Ketchup for blood

DISCUSSION:
God is a God of second chances. He gave Jonah a second chance to obey, the Ninevites a second chance, and He loves to forgive you and give you a second chance too (1 John 1:9).

REVIEW VERSE:
Jonah 2:1,10

1 Then Jonah prayed to the Lord his God from the fish's belly.

10 So the Lord spoke to the fish, and it vomited Jonah onto dry land.

SUMMARY:
Jonah was a prophet. God wanted him to preach to Nineveh. Jonah did not want to so he hopped on a boat and went the opposite way. The sea raged. The men drew lots and found that Jonah was the cause. They threw him overboard. Jonah was swallowed by a great fish. After three days and nights he was spit up onto the shore of Nineveh. He preached the truth. The people of Nineveh repented and God relented from the destruction he was going to do.

LESSON 47. MARY AND THE ANGEL
Luke 1:28-33

ACTIVITY:
Make an Angel ornament. Mix ingredients together and roll out mixture on a cutting board. Use an angel-shaped cookie cutter to cut out the shapes. Poke a hole through the top for a string or hook. Bake at 275 degrees for one hour. Paint and decorate when they are cool.

SUPPLIES:
- 1/3 cup water
- 1/2 cup salt
- 1 cup of flour
- Angel-shaped cookie cutter
- Acrylic paint (white or yellow or gold)

DISCUSSION:
Jesus was born of the Virgin Mary. His birth is a miracle. Why?

Jesus is fully God and fully man.

REVIEW VERSE:
Luke 1:28-33

> *28 And having come in, the angel said to her, "Rejoice, highly favored one, the Lord is with you; blessed are you among women!" 29 But when she saw him, she was troubled at his saying, and considered what manner of greeting this was. 30 Then the angel said to her, "Do not be afraid, Mary, for you have found favor with God. 31 And behold, you will conceive in your womb and bring forth a Son, and shall call His name JESUS. 32 He will be great, and will be called the Son of the Highest; and the Lord God will give Him the throne of His father David. 33 And He will reign over the house of Jacob forever, and of His kingdom there will be no end.*

SUMMARY:
At this time the Romans are now the ruling people of the Israelites. An angel appears to Mary and tells her she is going to have a baby. She is not going to conceive the normal way babies are conceived. This baby will be the one all the Jews were waiting for: The Messiah. His name would be called Jesus, which means God saves. Immanuel means God with us. Jesus is the one they were waiting for to save them.

LESSON 48. JESUS'S BIRTH
Luke 2:4-7

ACTIVITY:
Make an edible manger scene.

1. Get a plate

2. Spread peanut butter on it. (Peanut butter serves as the "glue.")

3. Get two graham cracker squares and put a little peanut butter on top to form a triangle for the stable.

4. You may use pretzels or graham crackers to make a manger.

5. Add the shredded wheat, breaking it apart for the hay in the manger.

6. Use the gummy bears as Mary and Joseph and Baby Jesus.

7. You may use frosting, decorating gel, or peanut butter for the swaddling clothes of Jesus.

8. Add peanut butter to the animal's feet so they can stand up.

9. Use decorating gel to make a star for the manger or clothes for the people. (You may include wise men and shepherds, too.)

SUPPLIES:
- Graham crackers
- Peanut butter or frosting
- Animal crackers or cookies
- Gummy bears
- Shredded mini wheats, plain or frosted
- Optional: decorating gel, pretzels
- Wrapped candy for the "treasures"

DISCUSSION:
It is an awesome thing that the Creator of the Universe, King of Kings chose to be born in a stable.

REVIEW VERSE:
Luke 2:4-7

4 Joseph also went up from Galilee, out of the city of Nazareth, into Judea, to the city of David, which is called Bethlehem, because he was of the house and lineage of David, 5 to be registered with Mary, his betrothed wife, who was with child. 6 So it was, that while they were there, the days were completed for her to be delivered. 7 And she brought forth her firstborn Son, and wrapped Him in swaddling cloths, and laid Him in a manger, because there was no room for them in the inn.

SUMMARY:
Mary and her husband to be Joseph had to go to their original home town for a census. This town for Joseph was Bethlehem. This is why Jesus was born in Bethlehem, yet raised in Nazareth. This is really amazing that the God of the universe is born in an animal's trough.

LESSON 49. THE SHEPHERDS
Luke 2:8-12

ACTIVITY:
Make a sheep. Use a popsicle stick and clothespins (you may paint them if you wish). Put the clothes pins on each side of the stick, with one side sticking out one inch for the head. Place it on the table so it stands up. Glue cotton on both sides of the sheep.

SUPPLIES:
- Clothespins
- Popsicle sticks
- Cotton
- Glue
- Optional: black or white paint, wobbly eyes

DISCUSSION:
The shepherds came to worship Jesus. Discuss why we should too.

REVIEW VERSE:
Luke 2: 8-12

> *8 Now there were in the same country shepherds living out in the fields, keeping watch over their flock by night. 9 And behold, an angel of the Lord stood before them, and the glory of the Lord shone around them, and they were greatly afraid. 10 Then the angel said to them, "Do not be afraid, for behold, I bring you good tidings of great joy which will be to all people. 11 For there is born to you this day in the city of David a Savior, who is Christ the Lord. 12 And this will be the sign to you: You will find a babe wrapped in swaddling cloths, lying in a manger."*

SUMMARY:
God choose to proclaim His Son's birth to lowly shepherds. They went to worship the new born king.

LESSON 50. SIMEON AND ANNA
Luke 2:26-32, 36-38

ACTIVITY:
Make a gift for Jesus. Have each person think what he or she would like to give to Jesus. What do you think Jesus would like to have from you?

Move the conversation away from "stuff" and think about things of the heart, such as: compassion (asking if our friends are okay if they get hurt), casting our burdens (telling Jesus when we are sad or are having a hard time), and forgiveness (telling Jesus we are sorry, before Mommy and Daddy tell us to).

SUPPLIES:
Gift wrap, paper

DISCUSSION:
What are some things we can we do to bless the heart of God?

REVIEW VERSE:
Luke 2:26-32, 36-38

> *26 And it had been revealed to him by the Holy Spirit that he would not see death before he had seen the Lord's Christ. 27 So he came by the Spirit into the temple. And when the parents brought in the Child Jesus, to do for Him according to the custom of the law, 28 he took Him up in his arms and blessed God and said: 29 "Lord, now You are letting Your servant depart in peace, according to Your word; 30 for my eyes have seen Your salvation 31 which You have prepared before the face of all peoples, 32 a light to bring revelation to the Gentiles, and the glory of Your people Israel."*

> *36 Now there was one, Anna, a prophetess, the daughter of Phanuel, of the tribe of Asher. She was of a great age, and had lived with a husband seven years from her virginity; 37 and this woman was a widow of about eighty-four years, who did not depart from the temple, but served*

God with fastings and prayers night and day. 38 And coming in that instant she gave thanks to the Lord, and spoke of Him to all those who looked for redemption in Jerusalem.

SUMMARY:
These two people are filled with joy being able to see with their own two eyes Israel's promised Messiah. Their long awaited Savior was here.

LESSON 51. WISE MEN
Matthew 2:7-11

ACTIVITY:
Make a star ornament.

1. Get 3 popsicle sticks. Glue the middles together forming an X and then a line through the X with the 3rd stick to make a star.

2. After the glue dries, paint the star. Add glitter and decorations.

3. Add string.

4. Allow one hour to dry.

SUPPLIES:
- Popsicle sticks
- Gold or yellow paint
- Glitter, or decorations like buttons, beads, or various jewels
- String

DISCUSSION:
Nothing should stop us from worshipping Jesus. What are some things that can get in the way? Why do we let that happen?

REVIEW VERSE:
Matthew 2:7-11

> 7 Then Herod, when he had secretly called the wise men, determined from them what time the star appeared. 8 And he sent them to Bethlehem and said, "Go and search carefully for the young Child, and when you have found Him, bring back word to me, that I may come and worship Him also." 9 When they heard the king, they departed; and behold, the star which they had seen in the East went before them, till it came and stood over where the young Child was. 10 When they saw the star, they rejoiced with exceedingly great joy. 11 And when they had come into the

house, they saw the young Child with Mary His mother, and fell down and worshiped Him. And when they had opened their treasures, they presented gifts to Him: gold, frankincense, and myrrh.

SUMMARY:
The Wise Men came from the east. They had studied the stars which had been passed down from generation to generation. They knew that a special king had been born. They came to worship this new king.

LESSON 52. WISE MEN ESCAPE
Matthew 2:12,16

ACTIVITY:
Play Hide and Seek.

The "wise men" are the hiders, "Herod" the seeker

The wise men find a place to hide

As soon as Herod finds the wise men, he falls to the ground.

SUPPLIES:
- None

DISCUSSION:
Herod did not want Jesus to take over his rule. We should not be like that. We should allow Jesus be the king of our lives, doing what he wants and not just what we want to do.

REVIEW VERSE:
Matthew 2:12,16

> *12 Then, being divinely warned in a dream that they should not return to Herod, they departed for their own country another way.*
>
> *16 Then Herod, when he saw that he was deceived by the wise men, was exceedingly angry; and he sent forth and put to death all the male children who were in Bethlehem and in all its districts, from two years old and under, according to the time which he had determined from the wise men.*

SUMMARY:
The wise men from the east assumed everyone in that area knew about this big event. The ruler at that time, Caesar Augustus, felt threatened by this new "king" he had decided to wipe out all the baby/toddler boys in the region. This is why he asked for

directions so he too could "worship", which was quite the opposite of his true intentions. The wise men were warned in a dream so they basically snuck out of the country without reporting to Caesar. Joseph was also warned and fled to Egypt until this ruler had died.

LESSON 53. ZECHERIAH
Luke 1:13

ACTIVITY:
Play "Guess What I'm Trying to Say." Parents should go first. They could draw a picture of themselves, a heart, and their child to say "Mommy loves Johnny," or take turns drawing whatever you would like. Everyone draws a picture of something and sees if the other person can guess what they are drawing without using any words or gestures, only the picture on the piece of paper.

SUPPLIES:
- Crayons
- Markers and a writing pad
- Optional: a white board, chalkboard, or magnetic writing board

DISCUSSION:
Don't ever forget that God is in control of life. Breathing, seeing, hearing, walking, talking—we do all of these things because He has allowed us to. Thank Jesus for all you have, all you can do, and all you are!

REVIEW VERSE:
Luke 1:13

> *13 But the angel said to him, "Do not be afraid, Zacharias, for your prayer is heard; and your wife Elizabeth will bear you a son, and you shall call his name John*

SUMMARY:
John the Baptist would be the famous son of Elizabeth and Zacharius. Elizabeth and Mary, Jesus mother, were cousins. John the Baptist was full of the Holy Spirit and prepared the way for the Lord, encouraging people to repent of their wicked ways and receive their Messiah, Jesus Christ. Zacharius was unable to speak, because of his lack of faith when he was told God was going to give him a child, until the child was born.

LESSON 54. JESUS LOST
Luke 2:49

ACTIVITY:
Play Hide and Seek, pretending to be Jesus and his parents. "Jesus" hides with a Bible in his hand. When his parents find him, they say "Where were you? We were so worried about you." "Jesus" replies "I was about my Father's business" (humbly, not cocky).

SUPPLIES:
- A Bible

DISCUSSION:
Jesus went with His parents as an example of his humble obedience even though he created his own parents. We should be like Jesus and obey our parents with a good attitude.

REVIEW VERSE:
Luke 2:49

> *49 And He said to them, "Why did you seek Me? Did you not know that I must be about My Father's business?"*

SUMMARY:
Even as a young man, Jesus found favor among men. The priest were amazed at His insight into scripture. I love Jesus response to His parents, "I must be about my Father's business." He was very focused on what his purpose in life was.

LESSON 55. JOHN THE BAPTIST
Matthew 3:13

ACTIVITY:
Baptize your stuffed animal.

SUPPLIES:
- Stuffed animal
- Pool or tub of water

DISCUSSION:
Explain that baptism is a symbol of what Jesus is doing inside our hearts.

REVIEW VERSE:
Matthew 3:13

> *13 Then Jesus came from Galilee to John at the Jordan to be baptized by him.*

SUMMARY:
John the Baptist was baptizing people all the time. Jesus, God in flesh, came to be baptized. Although, Jesus was perfect, He was baptized to "fulfill all righteousness". Baptism for us is an outward symbol of what goes on in our hearts once God reveals Himself to us. We recognize we are sinners and needing to be cleansed by Jesus. When we enter the water it is like we are "dying" to our natural way of doing things (sinful) and being raised up new into new life of living by the Spirit, doing things that please God.

LESSON 56. JESUS CALLS THE DISCIPLES
Luke 5:11

ACTIVITY:
Play Follow the Leader. This is a game where you make a line of people, one behind the other. The person in front leads everyone else under chairs, over benches. They can jump or turn around while they walk or walk silly. Everyone must do what the person in the front does. Each child should get a turn being the one in front: the leader.

SUPPLIES:
- None

DISCUSSION:
WWJD? Every day, we should ask the question "What Would Jesus Do?"

REVIEW VERSE:
Luke 5:11

> *11 So when they had brought their boats to land, they forsook all and followed Him.*

SUMMARY:
Jesus chose 12 men to invest in. They called them His disciples. Jesus walks right up to these men in this chapter in the midst of their jobs and asked them to "forsake all" and follow Him. Jesus is calling us to also "forsake all" and follow Him. Every day He wants us to ask the Him, how He would like us to spend our time, energy and money.

LESSON 57. WATER INTO WINE
John 2:11

ACTIVITY:
"Turn the Water into Wine." Without your kids seeing you, put powdered drink mix at the bottom of a pitcher. Pour clear water into the pitcher to make a new drink.

SUPPLIES:
- Gatorade Powder Mix, lemonade mix, or any powder mix drink or food coloring
- An opaque pitcher or cup tall enough not to see the bottom

DISCUSSION:
God cares about you, the little things and the big too. Talk to him about all your thoughts and feelings-He loves you so much!

REVIEW VERSE:
John 2:11

> *11 This beginning of signs Jesus did in Cana of Galilee, and manifested His glory; and His disciples believed in Him.*

SUMMARY:
This is Jesus first recorded miracle. He is at a wedding. They run out of wine. Mary, His mother, in so many words asks for a miracle. Jesus does indeed turn the water into wine.

LESSON 58. HOLE IN THE ROOF
Luke 5:23-24

ACTIVITY:
Discover what it felt like to be the paralyzed man. Put a child in the blanket and have two adults at the ends of the blanket. Swing the child back and forth and tell him you are taking him to see Jesus. When you are done swinging him back and forth, gently land him on a couch or bed. Explain to the kids how hard it must feel to be bound up unable to walk. This is how the paralyzed men felt: very sad and discouraged.

The child then jumps up and down and says "I'm Healed!"

SUPPLIES:
- Large Blanket
- Bed or couch

DISCUSSION:
Jesus is our Healer. Discuss some people who have been healed.

REVIEW VERSE:
Luke 5:23-24

> 23 Which is easier, to say, 'Your sins are forgiven you,' or to say, 'Rise up and walk'? 24 But that you may know that the Son of Man has power on earth to forgive sins"—He said to the man who was paralyzed, "I say to you, arise, take up your bed, and go to your house."

SUMMARY:
I love this account in the Bible. This man is in a pretty hopeless situation. His friends hear that this miracle worker is in town. They take their friend to see him. They are so persistent and passionate to see Jesus, they cut a hole in the roof and lower him down. The greatest miracle, according to Jesus, is not that this lame man will walk again, but that his sins are forgiven. God is always doing awesome things for us to show He does have the power to forgive

all sins we are ashamed of. Nobody jumps up and down when Jesus says his sins are forgiven. We so many times miss the real WOW and settle for the earthly and temporal things that we want accomplished. How about God's presence? That is a WOW we can have right now if we want it.

LESSON 59. SERMON ON THE MOUNT
Matthew 6:34

ACTIVITY:
Go bird watching/flower picking.

SUPPLIES:
- Bread
- Scissors

DISCUSSION:
Talk about how God promises to take care of us even better than birds and flowers, because he loves us so much more!

REVIEW VERSE:
Matthew 6:34

> *34 Therefore do not worry about tomorrow, for tomorrow will worry about its own things. Sufficient for the day is its own trouble.*

SUMMARY:
The Sermon on the Mount is a great teaching of Jesus on how to live a different more fulfilled life here on earth, which is of course thinking all about doing things that matter for eternity.

LESSON 60. THE CENTURION
Luke 7:9

ACTIVITY:
Place a special hat on a child. He is then Centurion for a Moment.

Each child gets to be the Centurion (boss) and give one command to the parent, and the parent does that one thing.

SUPPLIES:
- A special hat (a hat with authority attached, such as the armed forces, works well)

DISCUSSION:
Jesus has full authority. All He has to do is speak and what He says must be done.

REVIEW VERSE:
Luke 7:9

> *9 When Jesus heard these things, He marveled at him, and turned around and said to the crowd that followed Him, "I say to you, I have not found such great faith, not even in Israel!"*

SUMMARY:
There are many miracles in the Bible that correlate with faith. Sometimes Jesus even said, "Your faith has made you well." This does not necessarily mean that if we ask for a healing and do not receive it, that we don't have faith. But sometimes our lack of faith can affect us receiving all God has for us. Faith does, however, come by hearing the word of God. Faith does have to do with showing in our life, choices and actions that God is who He says He is and will do what He says He will do. The Centurion had faith that all Jesus had to do was speak the word. He had belief that Jesus had that much authority. So his actions left the servant at home, and had friends ask the Lord to heal this servant. He did not even see it necessary

for Him to lay hands on him. He believed Jesus had full authority to speak the words and it would be so. Whether God decides to heal the way we hope or not is one thing, expecting God to heal because He is the Healer and that's what He does and looking for how God is going to do it- is completely another story. God sometimes allows us to go through physical trials to heal us of much more damaging things like our destructive pride or selfishness and things of this nature.

LESSON 61. PARABLE OF THE SEED
Matthew 13:18

ACTIVITY:
Act out the parable of the seed.

The kids are the seeds, and a parent is the bird that pretends to eat the seeds. Another person pretends to be a rock.

The "seeds" (kids) try to get a drink, but the "rock" won't let them.

Another "seed" (child) pretends to choke. Talk about the weeds "choking out the seed," which is the Word of God.

Talk about good soil (dirt) that helps the "seeds" grow and grow and grow. Lift them higher and higher and higher and put them on your shoulders.

SUPPLIES:
- None

DISCUSSION:
God wants our heart to be soft, good soil that is ready to do what He says (share, be kind, say nice things, etc.)

What are some things that will choke out the word of God?

What happens when rocks are in the way of seeds?

What happens to a seed when the weeds in your yard grow? Does the seed have a chance to grow?

REVIEW VERSE:
Matthew 13:18

18 "Therefore hear the parable of the sower

SUMMARY:
Jesus interprets this story. He says the seed is the word of "the kingdom". This is the message of the Bible: Christ came into the world to forgive sinners of their sins, through His work on the cross so we can enter into His kingdom after we die. The people who don't really get it, who don't really see their desperate need of forgiveness, this powerful life changing truth to those does not go deep into their hearts, but it is snatched away by Satan and exchanged for his way; which is the pursuit of wealth. The stony ground are those who are excited about going to heaven, but do not really root themselves in the Lord, or cling to Jesus, these people when it gets hard, abandon a life for Christ. The thorny ground are those who hear it, receive it as their own, but basically get distracted by money and start to pursue getting wealth and not getting closer to Christ. This person is not very affective for the kingdom of God and has missed the purpose of their life. The fertile soil is every person who hears it, receives it, and really truly gets it, the truth is like a light bulb coming on and when this happens there is incredible productivity in drawing people to Christ, which He calls fruitfulness!

LESSON 62. PARABLE OF THE MUSTARD SEED
Matthew 13:31,32

ACTIVITY:
Plant a seed. Place dirt in a cut-off milk container. (You can use one carton for the group, or a carton for each child.) Plant your seed.

SUPPLIES:
- Seeds
- Dirt
- Half-gallon or quart milk carton (cut open)

DISCUSSION:
Let the child see the size of a mustard seed.

Discuss the verses at length. What did Jesus mean when he described the tiny seed?

It's hard to imagine that a seed so small would become a tree so large that birds could nest in the branches.

Why does Jesus make a difference in our lives?

REVIEW VERSE:
Matthew 13:31,32

> *31 Another parable He put forth to them, saying: "The kingdom of heaven is like a mustard seed, which a man took and sowed in his field, 32 which indeed is the least of all the seeds; but when it is grown it is greater than the herbs and becomes a tree, so that the birds of the air come and nest in its branches."*

SUMMARY:
Here is another picture of what faith is like. There is a moment in time, when we believe in Christ, and we became a brand new creation. We receive the Holy Spirit. This empowers us to do things far beyond what our minds can conceive and much larger and outside of ourselves. Being a part of what GOD is doing is huge, absolutely positively ginormous!!!!

LESSON 63. GOOD FISH/BAD FISH
Matthew 13:47-51

ACTIVITY:
Go "fishing."

Kids and parents can draw little fish on recloseable sandwich bags with a permanent marker. Without the kids watching, fill some of the bags with ice cream and some with moldy old food. (If you do not have anything moldy, make up something that looks gross.) Be sure the bags are sealed properly.

Fill the bathtub with cold water and enough dishwashing liquid to make bubbles. (You may want to do this ahead of time so the ice cream won't melt.) While the kids are distracted, put the bags into the water.

Kids then go "fishing," using the net to pull out all the "fish." They separate the good fish from the bad.

SUPPLIES:
- Plastic recloseable sandwich bags
- Permanent marker
- Individually wrapped ice cream
- Net (you can use a toy butterfly net from the dollar store)
- Dishwashing liquid

DISCUSSION:
One day Jesus will look at everyone's heart and separate the "good" (forgiven) hearts from the "bad" (unrepentant) hearts. The forgiven hearts love Jesus; the unforgiven hearts are the ones who did not repent of sin. It's important for Jesus to be involved in our lives. He wants to be. We just have to invite him in.

REVIEW VERSE:
Matthew 13:47-51

47 "Again, the kingdom of heaven is like a dragnet that was cast into the sea and gathered some of every kind, 48 which, when it was full, they drew to shore; and they sat down and gathered the good into vessels, but threw the bad away. 49 So it will be at the end of the age. The angels will come forth, separate the wicked from among the just, 50 and cast them into the furnace of fire. There will be wailing and gnashing of teeth."

51 Jesus said to them, "Have you understood all these things?"

They said to Him, "Yes, Lord."

SUMMARY:
I just want to emphasize the difference between a good fish and a bad fish. A good fish is someone who relies on Jesus Christ to forgive them of all their sins. It is not how many "good" things you do outweighing the "bad" things. The Bible in Romans 3, God makes it clear we are all "bad" fish and only reliance on Jesus and His work on the cross makes us "good". Ephesians 3:8&9 is a great verse that clarifies this even further.

LESSON 64. THE PEARL
Matthew 13:44-46

ACTIVITY:
Go on a treasure hunt. Each child writes on a slip of paper the treasures they have from/in Jesus. Put all these slips of paper in the treasure box. Without the kids knowing, put money in the box and hide the box. Tell the kids to go on a treasure hunt. Whoever finds the box is to share what's inside.

SUPPLIES:
- Paper
- Pencil
- Quarter or dollar for each child
- A box to serve as a treasure box

DISCUSSION:
Friendship with Jesus is the most valuable thing we can have.

Why is this true?

Would you like your friends to learn about this "treasure" who is Jesus?

Share some ways you might show others you treasure their friendship.

REVIEW VERSE:
Matthew 13:44-46

> *44 "Again, the kingdom of heaven is like treasure hidden in a field, which a man found and hid; and for joy over it he goes and sells all that he has and buys that field. 45 "Again, the kingdom of heaven is like a merchant seeking beautiful pearls, 46 who, when he had found one pearl of great price, went and sold all that he had and bought it."*

SUMMARY:
There is no greater thing on earth than knowing Jesus. He truly is a treasure. Jesus was the greatest treasure of God the Father, He valued us so much to give up what cost Him the most, so that we could be saved. He did this when we were God's enemies. We obviously are highly precious to God. We are His "pearl of great price" and He is ours, worth giving up everything to follow Him.

LESSON 65. WIND AND THE WAVES
Mark 4:41

ACTIVITY:
Go for a boat ride. The parent puts the child in the "boat" and pulls them around in the water. The child pretends to be Jesus asleep. Then the child says "Peace, be still."

SUPPLIES:
- Tub or pool of water
- Something to serve as a boat (like an ice chest)

DISCUSSION:
Even the wind and waves must obey Jesus.

Talk about how it felt to ride in the "boat."

Did it feel scary? Did the "boat" rock so you felt like you were going to fall out? (Hopefully they didn't tip over!)

REVIEW VERSE:
Mark 4:41

> *41 And they feared exceedingly, and said to one another, "Who can this be, that even the wind and the sea obey Him!"*

SUMMARY:
What was selected in the gospels, which tells of the life and ministry of Jesus, is very purposeful. This story shows that He is Lord of nature.

LESSON 66. WOMAN HEALED
Mark 5:33

ACTIVITY:
"Shock" each other and guess who did it!

This activity is best done on a windy day, or during the winter months.

Have one child pretend to be Jesus, and have another child rub their feet on a rug and then try to shock "Jesus." "Jesus" felt power leave from Him. The person who plays Jesus tries to guess who touched him

Or rub a balloon against some wool. Put the balloon on "Jesus"'s head to make his hair stick up.

SUPPLIES:
- Balloon
- Wool

DISCUSSION:
The woman heard that all you would have to do is to touch the Messiah's garment (clothes) and you would be healed. She had faith that what He said was true. That is all she did and was healed. Do you believe God's words are true?

REVIEW VERSE:
Mark 5:33

> *33 But the woman, fearing and tembling, knowing what had happened to her, came and fell down before Him and told Him the whole truth*

SUMMARY:
This woman, according to the law, was considered unclean. This meant she was suppose to be isolated from everyone else. She had faith that healing was such a powerful essence of Christ, that all she had to do was touch them hem of His garment to receive

what she needed to be healed. Many people were crowding around Jesus. Jesus knew something powerful had just taken place. He stopped and she fell at his feet. He acknowledged what had just taken place, and had her acknowledge it as well.

LESSON 67. JESUS FEEDS THE MULTITUDES
Matthew 14:19-21

ACTIVITY:
Have a picnic outdoors (indoors if the weather is bad.) Each person gets one food item and one large drink. The idea is to share everything. Do not use plates; just take a bite/piece and pass the container. If there are rolls, have everyone just tear off a piece and pass along the roll.

SUPPLIES:
- Dinner (take-out Chinese food would be fun)

DISCUSSION:
Jesus is the Bread of Life that always fills us so we are not hungry any more. If you think you don't have enough (enough toys, enough food, enough to drink, enough friends, enough good looks) talk with Jesus and read His love letter to you (the Bible). You will see you have all you really need and so much more. Just like the disciples looking at what they had, it didn't look like they had enough, but they soon found out that God multiplied what they had, and they had more than enough!

REVIEW VERSE:
Matthew 14:19-21

> *19 Then He commanded the multitudes to sit down on the grass. And He took the five loaves and the two fish, and looking up to heaven, He blessed and broke and gave the loaves to the disciples; and the disciples gave to the multitudes. 20 So they all ate and were filled, and they took up twelve baskets full of the fragments that remained. 21 Now those who had eaten were about five thousand men, besides women and children.*

LESSON 68. WALKING ON WATER
Matthew 14:22-33

ACTIVITY:
Who can walk on water? Get a plank and see who can walk across the water. Now see who can step from the plank to the water without sinking, only getting their feet wet!

SUPPLIES:
- Pool or tub of water
- A plank (board large enough for child to walk on)

DISCUSSION:
Jesus can do amazing things. He can do things no one else in the world can do. We can do things with His help that we could never do without Him.

REVIEW VERSE:
Matthew 14:22-33

> *Immediately Jesus made His disciples get into the boat and go before Him to the other side…24But the boat was now in the middle of the sea…for the wind was contrary.*

Matthew 26-33

> *26And when the disciples saw Him walking on the sea…33 Then those who were in the boat came and worshiped Him, saying "Truly You are the Son of God."*

SUMMARY:
Have you ever heard someone say "We'll I can't walk on water!" This expression comes from this amazing event in history. A storm is brewing and here comes Jesus, walking on the water. This has never happened before or since. Peter gets a whirl at it and walks on water briefly. Why does He do this? I have no idea. But sometimes it's fun to think of the possibilities. Maybe He wanted to show them what doing the impossible could look like. He purposefully wanted us to know this aspect about Himself- with God there is always that element of surprise!

LESSON 69. BLIND MAN
John 9:6&7

ACTIVITY:
Go outside. Add some water to dirt and make mud. Make mud pies.

SUPPLIES:
- Mud
- Old clothes

DISCUSSION:
Jesus touches each person in a unique, special way.

REVIEW VERSE:
John 9:1-5

> *9 Now as Jesus passed by, He saw a man who was blind from birth….5 As long as I am in the world, I am the light of the world.*

John 9:6&7

> *6 But that you may know that the Son of Man has power on earth to forgive sins"—then He said to the paralytic, "Arise, take up your bed, and go to your house." 7 And he arose and departed to his house.*

SUMMARY:
This is another thing Jesus does give sight to the blind, not just physically, but spiritually as well. Jesus is the light. When we read about His life, we can see how we don't measure up. This hopefully leads us broken and desperate for His forgiveness and more of Him living through us.

LESSON 70. THE TAX
Matthew 17:24-27

ACTIVITY:
Play "Find the Fish." Put two coins in the fish per game, one to keep and one to give away. Parent hides the fish in different places with water (pool, Jacuzzi, bathtub, sink, pitcher of water). When the fish is found they get to keep one coin, and give one away.

SUPPLIES:
- A Fish (fake or dead)
- Coins

DISCUSSION:
We may not like certain rules, but if they don't break God's law, keep them anyway. It makes Jesus happy when we respect our authorities (teachers, policemen, grandparents, babysitters, etc.). Explain "authority" to them if they do not understand the meaning of the word.

REVIEW VERSE:
Matthew 17:24-27

> *24 When they had come to Capernaum, those who received the temple tax came to Peter and said, "Does your Teacher not pay the temple tax?" 25 He said, "Yes." And when he had come into the house, Jesus anticipated him, saying, "What do you think, Simon? From whom do the kings of the earth take customs or taxes, from their sons or from strangers?" 26 Peter said to Him, "From strangers." Jesus said to him, "Then the sons are free. 27 Nevertheless, lest we offend them, go to the sea, cast in a hook, and take the fish that comes up first. And when you have opened its mouth, you will find a piece of money; take that and give it to them for Me and you."*

SUMMARY:
This is interesting that Christ puts this reference into scripture. Jesus is asked to pay a tax. Jesus could just pay it, but He pricks Peter's brain a little bit by asking if the sons of the king are exempt and they were. Jesus is king over all, owns everything, made everything, and everything is for Him. The truth of the matter is that Caesars and the Priests owe Him their whole life as well as everything they own. The sons of the King of Kings, which would be Peter a follower of Christ are in reality exempt. After Christ enlightens Peter to reality, He tells them to pay the tax for the sake of not offending, and not for the sake of "entitlement". The reality is the only one entitled to anything is God.

LESSON 71. THE GOOD SAMARITAN
Luke 10:36&37

ACTIVITY:
Minister to those who are in need. Ask your family, who do we know that really needs help right now, or is really sad or hurting? What would bless them the most?

Do it right now—make a craft, card, pick flowers, paint a picture, call them on the phone, pray for them, make them a meal, buy them groceries, say encouraging words, hang out with them, or give them money.

SUPPLIES:
- Paper
- Stickers
- Crayons
- Markers

DISCUSSION:
Ask Jesus to help you see who needs to be shown love. Then be brave enough to do it! Help the child recognize people in need.

Parents: this is a wonderful opportunity for you to set an example.

REVIEW VERSE:
Luke 10:36&37

> *36 So which of these three do you think was neighbor to him who fell among the thieves?"*
>
> *37 And he said, "He who showed mercy on him."*
>
> *Then Jesus said to him, "Go and do likewise."*

SUMMARY:
This is a classic parable. A man asks Jesus how he can obtain eternal life. Jesus asks him what his understanding of scripture is. The man answers basically love God and love your neighbor as yourself. Jesus said, "Do this and you will live." And the man asks, "Who is my neighbor?" Then Jesus gives him this parable about priests and other righteous men who pass by this man in need. Then he purposefully chooses a Samaritan, a people who the Jews did not like, as a hero. The question then becomes a rather painful one "What kind of neighbor are you?" God really gets him to examine his heart, and if we are honest, our hearts, without divine intervention, are bent on doing things our own way instead of God's way, being merciful. If the man were to answer this honestly he would say, "I am a horrible, selfish neighbor." He then could humbly ask God, "But can you help me be like you?" The truth of the matter is: apart from being connected to God by having Him live in us and reign in us through Jesus Christ by His work on the cross, we can do no good thing!

LESSON 72. MARY AND MARTHA
Luke 10:38-42

ACTIVITY:
Have the child spend five minutes alone with God in their own quiet spot. (For the little ones, have them draw a picture of their day, especially their feelings today.) Then have them think about what Jesus would say about their day. You can help them along, hearing the voice of God by referring their thoughts back to what God's Word says (Psalm 139, Jeremiah 29:11, 1 Peter 5:7, John 3: 16).

SUPPLIES:
- Paper
- Pencil
- Bible, if they are old enough
- Journal, if they have one
- Worship song

DISCUSSION:
Jesus loves to hear you pray, but he also wants to speak with you (John 10:4). Teach them how to listen to the quiet voice in their heart. Help them learn the difference between their own thoughts and the impressions the Holy Spirit may want to stir. Whatever we receive in our thoughts from our spirit must always be in alignment with the Word of God.

REVIEW VERSE:
Luke 10:38-42

> *38 Now it happened as they went that He entered a certain village; and a certain woman named Martha welcomed Him into her house. 39 And she had a sister called Mary, who also sat at Jesus' feet and heard His word. 40 But Martha was distracted with much serving, and she approached Him and said, "Lord, do You not care that my sister has left me to serve alone? Therefore tell her to help me." 41 And Jesus answered*

and said to her, "Martha, Martha, you are worried and troubled about many things. 42 But one thing is needed, and Mary has chosen that good part, which will not be taken away from her."

SUMMARY:

Martha is working hard serving everyone. Mary is at the feet of Jesus, absorbing all she can of who He is and all she can learn from Him. When Martha asks Jesus to get Mary to help out, His reply is something like this: Mary has chosen to be with me, it is the only thing anyone needs, and I won't ask her to do something less important.

LESSON 73. HEALING ON THE SABBATH
Luke 13:13

ACTIVITY:
Be a "Rebel with a Cause." Do something kind on Sunday. Decide the details of what you will do together.

SUPPLIES:
- Decide that as a family

DISCUSSION:
Don't make excuses to not be kind: "I'm too tired," "I'm too busy," "It's too hard," "I don't want to," "But that's my favorite toy and I'm sure Grandma doesn't want me to share it with you because you might break it," etc. Be kind always.

REVIEW VERSE:
Luke 13:13

> *13 And He laid hands on her and immediately she was made straight, and glorified God.*

SUMMARY:
The Sabbath was on Saturday. God created it as a day of rest. It was against the law of the Jews (the Old Testament of the Bible) to do any work on the Sabbath. When the Pharisees, the religious leaders of this time, saw Jesus heal on the Sabbath, they accused Him of breaking "the Law". Jesus silenced them by reminding them how they helped their own animals out of pits on the Sabbath, and people have much more value to God than animals. So it was good to show kindness, by healing someone on the Sabbath. The Pharisees had no further argument.

LESSON 74. THE PARABLE OF THE LOST SHEEP
Luke 15:7

ACTIVITY:
Play hide and seek. Gather all your stuffed animals in a pile. One child picks one animal to hide. The other child/children "seekers" then look at the animals to find out which one is missing, and they see who can find it.

SUPPLIES:
- Stuffed Animals

DISCUSSION:
Jesus is like that good shepherd who will always come after us. He wants to forgive and be close to us. It makes Him sad when we wander away and don't like hanging out with Him. Jesus the good shepherd knows it's safer in His care than where wolves and lions might devour us (wanting too many "things", watching or playing violent games and movies).

REVIEW VERSE:
Luke 15:7

> *7 I say to you that likewise there will be more joy in heaven over one sinner who repents than over ninety-nine just persons who need no repentance.*

SUMMARY:
This parable communicates the heart of God. God's biggest desire is for us to "come to repentance". During our life time He will pursue us, try to get our attention, call us, and much more. He wants all people to have a right relationship with Him. He wants to forgive us our sins. This is repentance: seeing our need for God by seeing how far we miss the target. God helps us see the destructiveness of sin, and by the power of the Holy Spirit gives us the grace to have a productive, abundant, and free life.

LESSON 75. THE LOST COIN
Luke 15:8-10

ACTIVITY:
Have a scavenger hunt. The parents hide chocolate gold coins all over the house, and the children see how many they can find. (You can also unwrap one coin and put a dollar coin in that one.)

SUPPLIES:
- Chocolate gold coins

DISCUSSION:
As passionately as you searched for that coin, Jesus is just as passionate for you to go to Heaven and be with Him one day.

REVIEW VERSE:
Luke 15:8-10

> *8 "Or what woman, having ten silver coins, if she loses one coin, does not light a lamp, sweep the house, and search carefully until she finds it? 9 And when she has found it, she calls her friends and neighbors together, saying, 'Rejoice with me, for I have found the piece which I lost!' 10 Likewise, I say to you, there is joy in the presence of the angels of God over one sinner who repents."*

SUMMARY:
This is another parable that shows us God's heart for us. When we lose something we really need, we are very passionate about finding it, like the lost coin in this story. We are very valuable to God. He wants us to know His heart: He is consumed with thoughts of you and passionately desires to spend eternity with you.

LESSON 76. THE PRODIGAL SON
Luke 15:32

ACTIVITY:
Have a pretend "Welcome Home Party."

The child "runs away" in the backyard, upstairs, or down the street with another parent. Then the child comes back home. When the father sees him, he runs to hug him, greet him, gives him the royal coat, and invites him in for a big party.

SUPPLIES:
- A cake
- Party supplies

DISCUSSION:
Have them explain what it felt like when they reenacted the story. How did they feel when they ran away? Did they feel special and loved when the father welcomed them back home? Was the father angry when his young son returned? Talk about God's never-ending love for us.

REVIEW VERSE:
Luke 15:32

> *32 It was right that we should make merry and be glad, for your brother was dead and is alive again, and was lost and is found.*

SUMMARY:
This is another classic parable Jesus tells. A son wants his inheritance. He runs away and squanders it. He has nothing and "comes to his senses" realizing how good he had it with his father. He comes back home, embarrassed of all he had done. My favorite part of this story is while his son was a long way of, the father runs to him embraces him, warmly receives him and treats him like royalty. It is so embarrassing to have to come to Jesus needing forgiveness for the things you do that are so unlike Him. But God obviously wants us to know, how He wants to forgive and the warmth He has. I expect harshness, but I get a hug instead. If I was God, I would want to never see my face again, but God runs to me like He can't wait to be with me. I guess all I can say, is I don't fully understand God's love for me, but I am very thankful for it!

LESSON 77. THE TEN LEPERS
Luke 17:18&19

ACTIVITY:
How many things can you be thankful for in a minute? Have two people hold a six foot piece of string. Another person says what they are thankful for. They get one clothespin to clip on the string per each statement.

SUPPLIES:
- Clothespins
- String

DISCUSSION:
How many lepers were healed? How many returned thanks to Jesus?

Is it hard to think of things to be thankful for?

Discuss the beautiful things around them to help them understand the things we often simply take for granted (the moon, stars, sun, darkness, ocean, sand, rain, wind, trees, birds, butterflies, etc.).

Tell God we're sorry we forget to say thank you! (We all do.)

REVIEW VERSE:
Luke 17:18&19

> *18 Were there not any found who returned to give glory to God except this foreigner?" 19 And Jesus said to him, " Arise, go your way Your faith has made you well."*

SUMMARY:
10 lepers ask Jesus to make them well. One returns to worship Jesus and give thanks. This is an important reminder to really thank God for all that He has done. He is good all the time, sometimes he allows bad things to happen, but if He does, it's always for a good purpose. No matter what trial we face, we always have something to be thankful to God for. We can always be thankful for salvation. He made a way for us to spend eternity with Him. God sacrificed a lot for us to make this happen.

LESSON 78. JESUS AND THE CHILDREN
Psalm 127:3. Luke 18:15-17

ACTIVITY:
Enjoy your children—just have fun with them for this activity. Some ideas: hug them; swing them around; wrestle with them; tickle them; play "the claw"; give them horsy rides; kiss them; make one super-large banana split, tie your hands behind your back, and dig in; make a tent with sheets or blankets, get flashlights, and make nighttime noises and tell stories with shadow puppets.

SUPPLIES:
- None

DISCUSSION:
This is a discussion between Mom, Dad and the Lord—away from little ears. Children are a gift from the Lord! Does your gift from God bug you, cramp your style, or wear you out? Ask Jesus for His eyes to see them the way He does. Ask the Lord for the strength to treasure their innocence, wonderment, free spirits, sweet and tender moments, their beauty, their eagerness to learn new things, etc. You might need to ask God and maybe your kids for forgiveness if you have been short, impatient, unkind, or quick to become angry.

REVIEW VERSE:
PS 127:3. Luke 18:15-17

3 Behold, children are a heritage from the LORD, The fruit of the womb is a reward.

SUMMARY:
There was something about Jesus that children were drawn to Him. I feel convicted by the Holy Spirit when they don't meet my expectations and I communicate irritation and harshness. I am so glad God is not like me. He is patient and understanding. He delights in His children. I want to communicate more delight in my kids instead

of "Get away from me." I want to do this in my tone of voice, my facial expressions, my attitude, my words, and my actions. I certainly need God to do this! My kids first impression of what God is like will be how my husband and I am towards them. This is a sobering thought.

LESSON 79. BLIND BARTIMAEUS
Luke 10:51&52

ACTIVITY:
Play "Lead the Blind." Blindfold one person; the other one leads the "blind" through a certain obstacle course. Take turns. Make an obstacle course using chairs to crawl through, canned goods to walk in and out of, blown-up balloons to walk through, a bucket of water to step over, or your own creative ideas.

SUPPLIES:
- Blindfold

DISCUSSION:
What did Bartimaeus say to Jesus? What did Jesus do for Bartimaeus?

REVIEW VERSE:
Luke 10:51&52

51 So Jesus answered and said to him, "What do you want Me to do for you?"

The blind man said to Him, "Rabboni, that I may receive my sight."

52 Then Jesus said to him, "Go your way; your faith has made you well." And immediately he received his sight and followed Jesus on the road.

SUMMARY:
This blind man was very insistent to get Jesus' attention. He did not care what others thought of him, he was silenced by those around him. Through all this, he still shouted to get God's attention. Jesus healed him. We should learn from this man's persistence, when we are inquiring of the Lord.

LESSON 80. ZACCHEUS
Luke 19:9

ACTIVITY:
Climb a tree. (Act out the story if you wish.)

SUPPLIES:
- A tree

DISCUSSION:
What are you willing to do, or even give up, because you love Jesus?

Talk about Zaccheus, his feelings, and his change of heart.

REVIEW VERSE:
Luke 19:9

> *9 And Jesus said to him, "Today salvation has come to this house, because he also is a son of Abraham;*

SUMMARY:
Zaccheus was a tax collector for the Romans. He was known for being dishonest to get rich. He climbs up a tree to get a glimpse of Jesus. Jesus invites himself over to Zaccheus' house. Zaccheus, in front of Jesus, gives half his wealth to the poor. Jesus proclaims that salvation had come to his house. This was obviously not a show, but a real heart change and Jesus recognized that. When Jesus comes into our heart, who we are, there is a dramatic change. We see the wrong we have done, and desire to make it right. Pleasing the Lord becomes our new goal in life.

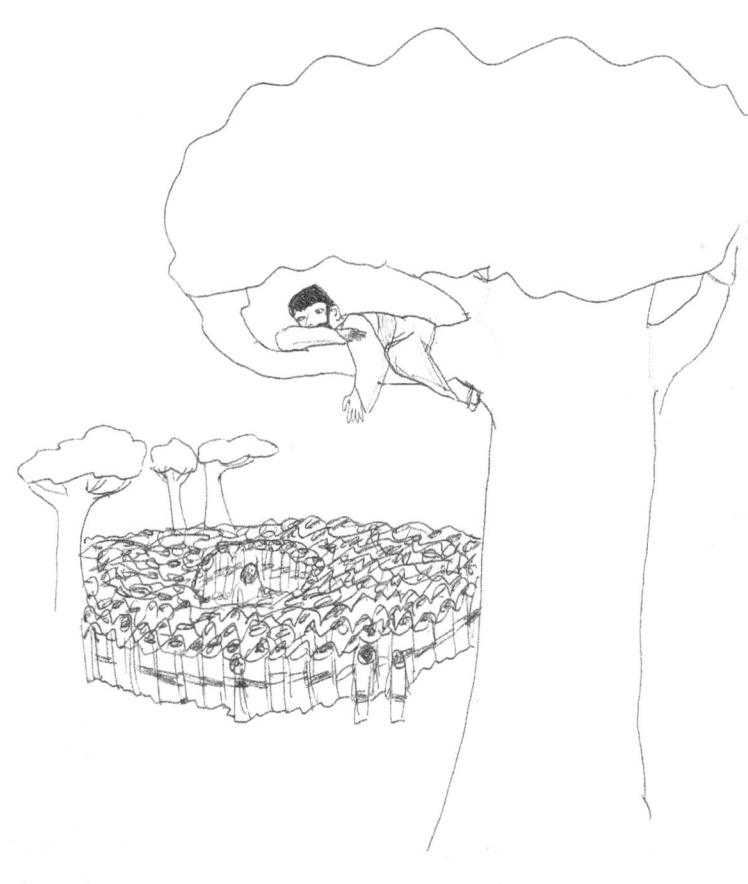

LESSON 81. THE WIDOW'S MITE
Mark 12:41-44

ACTIVITY:
"Surprise!"

The kids think of doing something kind for their parents as a surprise (try to do it sneaky without parents knowing). Some ideas for suprises are: dust, pickup around the house, make a peanut butter and jelly sandwich, make a card, perform a song for them. Parents can go outside or into another room until the kids are done with their "surprise." After all of them have done their deed, the kids invite the parents back to figure out the surprise. Then, parents surprise the kids with a treat.

SUPPLIES:
- A thank-you treat or reward (but don't let them know you are going to surprise them when you ask them to do this activity).

DISCUSSION:
Be kind, share, and do the right thing all the time with all your heart for Jesus—not like the Pharisees who only did things in front of others to look good.

REVIEW VERSE:
Mark 12:41-44

> *41 Now Jesus sat opposite the treasury and saw how the people put money into the treasury. And many who were rich put in much. 42 Then one poor widow came and threw in two mites, which make a quadrans. 43 So He called His disciples to Himself and said to them, "Assuredly, I say to you that this poor widow has put in more than all those who have given to the treasury; 44 for they all put in out of their abundance, but she out of her poverty put in all that she had, her whole livelihood."*

SUMMARY:
Jesus draws attention to this widow, who would normally have been overlooked. It is a good reminder that God sees what we do to honor Him. He sees the sacrifices we make. He sees our heart. He notices us.

LESSON 82. THE POOL OF BETHESDA
Luke 5:8&9

ACTIVITY:
Blow bubbles. Dump bubble solution on a waterproof table. Pass out the straws. Put them perpendicular to the table and blow through the straw.

Or, put bubble solution on your finger. Blow bubbles through a bubble blower. Try to catch them.

SUPPLIES:
- Bottle of bubbles or liquid dish soap
- Straws

DISCUSSION:
God never sleeps or slumbers, He is always there to listen, and is always working on people's hearts and in their lives. The bubbles only last for a brief moment. Discuss how God never leaves or forsakes us.

REVIEW VERSE:
Luke 5:8&9

> 8 When Simon Peter saw it, he fell down at Jesus' knees, saying, "Depart from me, for I am a sinful man, O Lord!"
>
> 9 For he and all who were with him were astonished at the catch of fish which they had taken;

SUMMARY:
There was a pool at Bethesda where many crippled and sick people went. An angel of the Lord would cause these waters to move and those who made it first into it, would be made well. This particular man did not have a friend to help him get to the water. Jesus made Him well. Jesus is a healer and a friend.

LESSON 83. MARY ANOINTS THE FEET OF JESUS WITH PERFUME
John 12:3

ACTIVITY:
Give each other a foot-rub. Wipe the lotion off with the towel so the child does not slip on a hardwood/tile/linoleum floor.

SUPPLIES:
- Lotion, perfume
- Towel

DISCUSSION:
We should give the best of our time, talents, and possessions—not the leftovers. When your brother or sister would like to play with something, share the best with them. When you do that because you love Jesus, you are giving the best.

REVIEW VERSE:
John 12:3

> 3 Then Mary took a pound of very costly oil of spikenard, anointed the feet of Jesus, and wiped His feet with her hair. And the house was filled with the fragrance of the oil.

SUMMARY:
Judas thought it was a waste to dump the expensive oil on Jesus' feet. Jesus honors her in front of everyone. Jesus is worth giving our best to.

LESSON 84. THE TRIUMPHAL ENTRY
John 12:12-15

ACTIVITIES:
Act out the story in the Bible verse. First, pretend to be a donkey, then grab a branch while shouting or singing "Hosanna." The parent can be the donkey. Some kids can wave the palm branches. One child can pretend to be Jesus riding on the donkey (parent's back).

SUPPLIES:
- Branches

DISCUSSION:
When people shouted "Hosanna," they were saying that Jesus was the Messiah—the king they were waiting a long time for.

REVIEW VERSE:
John 12:12-15

> *12 The next day a great multitude that had come to the feast, when they heard that Jesus was coming to Jerusalem, 13 took branches of palm trees and went out to meet Him, and cried out: "Hosanna! 'Blessed is He who comes in the name of the LORD!' The King of Israel!" 14 Then Jesus, when He had found a young donkey, sat on it; as it is written: 15 "Fear not, daughter of Zion; behold, your King is coming, sitting on a donkey's colt."*

SUMMARY:
Jesus is the King of the Jews, but not like any king the Jews had ever experience. He is the maker of heaven and earth who came to earth as a man, but very nature God. He makes His entrance just the opposite of the grandeur He deserves. He comes in as a humble king, on a donkey. The people shout "Hosanna". This is their way of proclaiming Him as the Savior they were waiting for.

LESSON 85. WASHING FEET
John 13:15

ACTIVITY:
Put water in a dishpan or tub with a squirt of dishwashing liquid. Parent can demonstrate to the child first. Each child has a turn to wash and dry the feet of another.

SUPPLIES:
- A towel
- Tub or old dishpan with soapy water

DISCUSSION:
Becoming the greatest in God's eyes by being the best servant we can be!

REVIEW VERSE:
John 13:15

> *15 For I have given you an example, that you should do as I have done to you.*

SUMMARY:
Jesus does this amazing act of servant-leadership by washing the disciple's feet. Jesus is their Lord, yet He bends down to serve them. He declares them all, except Judas, to be "clean". But every day we need to be cleansed by the Word. Jesus encouraged them to follow His example of setting out to serve others not to be served!

LESSON 86. THE LAST SUPPER
Matthew 26:26-28

ACTIVITY:
Explain or do Communion (if your kids have a relationship with Jesus).

SUPPLIES:
- Bread and grape juice (or wine for the adults)

DISCUSSION:
Explain how the bread is a symbol of Jesus being the bread of life.

His body was broken for us. Explain how the wine is the symbol of the blood that poured out on the cross to forgive us.

REVIEW VERSE:
Matthew 26:26-28

26 And as they were eating, Jesus took bread, blessed[a] and broke it, and gave it to the disciples and said, "Take, eat; this is My body."

27 Then He took the cup, and gave thanks, and gave it to them, saying, "Drink from it, all of you. 28 For this is My blood of the new[b] covenant, which is shed for many for the remission of sins.

SUMMARY:
Jesus takes a piece of bread and breaks it and says this is His body broken for them. Then takes the wine and declares that this is His blood poured out for them. He tells them to do this in remembrance of Him. When we take communion, breaking bread and drinking the "wine", we do this to remember what He did on the cross for us. God wants us to examine our hearts and make sure we are right with Him. This is a good time to confess any known sin and tell God how much you appreciate what He has done.

LESSON 87. THE CRUCIFIXION
John 19:17&18

SUPPLIES:
- Two Popsicle sticks, or sticks from outside
- String
- Band-aids

ACTIVITY:
Make a cross with two sticks. Use the string to tie it around where it intersects. Put the Band aids on the sticks to demonstrate how Jesus hurt for us.

DISCUSSION:
The cross should remind us of what Jesus did for us. Talk about what the cross means. Help them understand the meaning of the crucifixion.

REVIEW VERSE:
John 19:17&18

> *17 And He, bearing His cross, went out to a place called the Place of a Skull, which is called in Hebrew, Golgotha, 18 where they crucified Him, and two others with Him, one on either side, and Jesus in the center*

SUMMARY:
This is an impossible event in history to summarize. Jesus died on the cross. All the sacrifices the Jews were required to do in the Old Testament were a fore shadow of the ultimate sacrifice that would be made in the future, this one. Jesus stated on the cross "It is finished". This means that all that is needed to be done to forgive the world of their offenses against God was completed on the cross by Him alone. There is nothing else that is needed for us to be saved. Jesus was and is perfect, he "knew no sin". He is the perfect "lamb" that takes away our sins. The Bible says that "without the shedding of blood, there can be no forgiveness of sins." The sacrifices that the Jews made in the past were not good enough to take away all the wrong things they had done, but this one of Jesus bleeding to death on the cross is.

LESSON 88. RESURRECTION
Matthew 28:5&6

SUPPLIES:
- Mixing bowl
- 1 cup of whole pecans
- 1 tsp vinegar
- 3 egg whites
- Pinch of salt
- 1 cup of sugar
- Zip-lock baggie
- Piece of tape

ACTIVITY and DISCUSSION:
Make a Resurrection Cookie. This is an overnight activity.
Explain to the kids they have to wait to get the treat,
like the disciples had to wait for the resurrection.

Preheat the oven to 300 degrees.

1. Put pecans in the baggie. Beat them.
   Jesus was beaten by the Roman soldiers. John 19:1-3

2. Smell the vinegar. Put in the mixing bowl.
   Jesus was offered this to drink on the cross. John 19:28-30

3. Add egg whites to the bowl. Eggs represent life.
   Jesus us gave His life to give us eternal life. John 10:10-11

4. Add the salt. Let each child taste a little salt.
   It represents the tears He shed in Gethsemane. Matthew 26:36-46

5. Add 1 cup of sugar. Let child taste grains of sugar.
   The sweetest part of this story is that He died,
   because He loves us so much John 3:16

6. Adult: beat with a mixer until stiff peaks form.
   The white is for the purity and cleanliness we have when
   we ask Jesus to forgive us our sins. Isaiah 1:18

7. Fold in the broken nuts. Put wax paper on a cookie sheet.
   Drop mounds onto wax paper to represent
   the rocky tomb for Jesus. Matt.27:57-60

8. Put cookie sheet in the oven. Turn the oven off.
   Give each child tape to seal the oven shut (wear oven mitts
   please). The tomb was sealed shut Matthew 27:65-66

9. Go to bed. It is sad to leave the cookies.
   The disciples were sad to leave Jesus. John 16:20, 22

   Leave the cookies in the oven overnight.

10. On the first Easter everyone was
    surprised that the tomb was empty.

    Take a bite of the cookie. They are empty inside
    just like the tomb. HE IS RISEN! Matt. 28:1-9

REVIEW VERSES:
Matthew 28:5&6

> *5 And the angel answered and said to the women, "Do not be afraid, for I know that you seek Jesus who was crucified. 6 "He is not here; for He is risen, as He said. Come, see the place where the Lord lay.*

SUMMARY:
This is also very crucial to testimony of Jesus. He claimed He would rise from the dead. If He did not, He would not be truthful, just another man claiming to be the "Savior of the World". He is the first to rise from the dead and remains alive still. He conquered the grave. No man has the power to defeat death, only the God/Man Jesus Christ!

LESSON 89. JESUS AND THE FISH
John 21:7

ACTIVITY:
Make s'mores. Have a camp-out too if you wish and toast marshmallows to make s'mores. Or you can assemble s'mores and do a quick "zap" in the microwave to soften the chocolate and marshmallows.

SUPPLIES:
- Graham crackers
- Chocolate bar
- Marshmallows

DISCUSSION:
Think of that commercial "What would you do for a Klondike bar?"

What crazy thing might you do if you saw Jesus? (If the kids are older they can write their answers.) Either way, their responses might be worth keeping.

REVIEW VERSES:
John 21:7

> *7 Therefore that disciple whom Jesus loved said to Peter, "It is the Lord!" Now when Simon Peter heard that it was the Lord, he put on his outer garment (for he had removed it), and plunged into the sea.*

SUMMARY:
This is a miracle and appearance of Jesus after He had risen from the dead. Jesus helps the men catch fish. This is very symbolic of what the disciples would do. Jesus said He would make them "fishers of men." After Jesus ascends to the clouds, they become filled with the Holy Spirit just a short time later. They preached to Jews and Non-Jews, who were called Gentiles, telling them the good news that they can go to heaven because of what Jesus had done on the cross and He rose from the grave to prove all that He said was true.

LESSON 90. ASCENSION
Acts 1:9

ACTIVITY:
What do you think the sky looked like when Jesus ascended? Use blue paper or let them draw a blue sky. Glue cotton balls to the blue sky. Draw a picture on the paper of Jesus ascending into the clouds.

Puffy clouds are called cumulus, wispy clouds are called cirrus, and clouds that look like steps are called stratus.

SUPPLIES:
- Cotton
- Paper
- Crayons

DISCUSSION:
Who are you going to tell about Jesus? Pray first so you can make the most of every opportunity to tell and show others about Christ. Pray for the people you know that don't know Jesus loves them yet!

REVIEW VERSE:
Acts 1:9

> *9 Now when He had spoken these things, while they watched, He was taken up, and a cloud received Him out of their sight*

SUMMARY:
The disciples witnessed Jesus going all the way up to the clouds, until they could not see Him any longer. Jesus is a living Savior.

LESSON 91. PENTECOST & FRUIT OF THE SPIRIT
Acts 2:1,2 & Galatians 5:22&23

ACTIVITY:
Have the kids wait for "The Gift." Inside the box, put a piece of fruit as a symbol of the fruit of the Holy Spirit. (Carve the corresponding fruit of the spirit onto the fruit, see below, or write the word on masking tape and stick it onto the fruit, but do not write directly on the fruit.) You can also get nine different fruits for all the fruit of God's Spirit (Galatians 5:22). Celebrate the Gift we have—being filled with the Holy Spirit. Make a special dessert with that special gift (fruit).

SUPPLIES:
- Wrapping Paper
- Box
- Fruit
- Caramel dip, candy apple mix, or banana split supplies

DISCUSSION:
Talk about the difference the Holy Spirit can make in our life.

REVIEW VERSE:
Acts 2:1,2

> *1 When the Day of Pentecost had fully come, they were all with one accord in one place. 2 And suddenly there came a sound from heaven, as of a rushing mighty wind, and it filled the whole house where they were sitting.*

Galatians 5:22&23

> *22 But the fruit of the Spirit is love, joy, peace, longsuffering, kindness, goodness, faithfulness, 23 gentleness, self-control. Against such there is no law.*

SUMMARY:
When we ask Jesus to forgive us our sins, and ask Him to be the boss of our life, He fills us with the Holy Spirit. As we grow closer to Him we have more of His fruit in our life. If you're able to get these fruits, this will help your kids memorize the fruit of God's Spirit.

Love: *A Red Apple*
It almost looks like a heart.

Joy: *Blueberry*
This was inspired by Madame Blueberry from Veggie Tales. She was very "blue" until she became more thankful for what she had, instead of always wanting more.

Peace: *Pear*
It takes a PAIR of people getting along to have peace. It pleases God to put other's first and not demand your own way.

Patience: *Orange*
It takes a lot of patience to peel an orange. God wants us to be patient with others, give them time to accomplish things or to understand.

Kindness: *Watermelon*
I think of picnics with friends or family when I am eating a watermelon. If you see someone all alone, be kind, hang out with them. Be their friend. Have a picnic.

Goodness: *Banana*
A banana has a lot of goodness in it. It has potassium which helps your body function correctly. God helps us function correctly!

Faithfulness: *Grapes*
God wants us to be connected to Him. A branch of grapes to be needs to be connected to the vine in order to grow its fruit. This is called faithfulness, staying connected. It is also important to stay connected with other believers to help us keep on following Him.

Gentleness: *Peach*
A peach is soft and fuzzy. God wants our responses to be soft and not harsh or quick-tempered.

Self-Control: *Coconut*
This was inspired by almost getting clobbered by a coconut in Costa Rica. There are times people are not very cool, we may want to clobber them with a coconut even with our words, but it is good to avoid being mean and have self-control and hold back.

LESSON 92. THE BEGGAR
Acts 9:3-5

ACTIVITY:
Sing a Christian song with lots of jumping or a massive "mosh-pit" for the older ones. Here's an oldie but goody:

Silver and Gold have I none
Such as I have, give I thee
In the name of Jesus Christ
Of Nazareth rise up and walk
And they were walking, and leaping and praising God
(Repeat twice.)
In the name of Jesus Christ
Of Nazareth rise up and walk!

SUPPLIES:
- Favorite "jumping" Christian song

DISCUSSION:
The name of Jesus Christ is powerful, that's why we say "In the name of Jesus" in our prayers. We don't say "In the name of Sally or Tommy." That would be silly. Jesus name is above all names. All power and authority has been given Him by God the Father.

REVIEW VERSE:
Acts 9:3-5

> *3 As he neared Damascus on his journey, suddenly a light from heaven flashed around him. 4 He fell to the ground and heard a voice say to him, "Saul, Saul, why do you persecute me?"*
>
> *5 "Who are you, Lord?" Saul asked.*
>
> *"I am Jesus, whom you are persecuting," he replied.*

SUMMARY:
It was amazing the miracles the disciples did in the name of Jesus. Many people were coming to repentance and receiving Christ, yet there was much persecution from Jesus' own people the Jewish religious leaders at this time.

LESSON 93. SAUL
Acts 9:1-19

ACTIVITY:
Play flashlight tag. One child is Saul and finds a place to hide in the dark (indoors or outdoors). The others have flashlights and try to find him. When Saul is found, throw him the blindfold to use and lead him "home" to his bed.

SUPPLIES:
- Flashlight(s)
- Blindfold

DISCUSSION:
The power of Jesus can change who we are—from mean to kind, from selfish to sharing.

REVIEW VERSE:
Acts 9:1-4

> 1 Then Saul, still breathing threats…4 Then he fell to the ground and heard….kick against the goads.

Acts 9:7-19

> 7 And the men who journeyed…19 So when he had received food, he was strengthened. Then Saul spent some days with the disciples at Damascus.

SUMMARY:
God revealed Himself to Saul in an amazing way. Saul is persecuting the new Christians and was condoning the death of Stephen the first "martyr recorded in the Bible. A bright light appears and it is Jesus asking why Saul is persecuting Him. Jesus takes it personal when anyone hurts the church, those who accept Him as their Lord and Savior. Saul becomes blind and receives

sight from a follower of Christ who knows Saul as someone who is trying to kill him. This follower, Ananias, prays for Saul and he receives his sight and becomes this on fire missionary, evangelist, for Christ. He becomes known as Paul the Apostle.

LESSON 94. PAUL AND SILAS
Acts 16:25&26

ACTIVITY:
Act this story out. All the kids are Paul and Silas. They walk around talking to each other about Jesus. They get sent to prison because of it (parents drag them to a homemade jail cell). All the kids sing as loud and joyfully as they can—the parents are the earthquake that causes the doors to fly open. Everyone is free.

SUPPLIES:
- A homemade "prison" (like an old large cardboard box)

DISCUSSION:
Amazing things can happen when we praise God with all our heart.

Talk about this story. Ask them how it felt when they were in prison and how free it felt to be out of the box (if you choose to use one).

REVIEW VERSE:
Acts 16:25&26

> *25 But at midnight Paul and Silas were praying and singing hymns to God, and the prisoners were listening to them. 26 Suddenly there was a great earthquake, so that the foundations of the prison were shaken; and immediately all the doors were opened and everyone's chains were loosed*

SUMMARY:
Paul, who has just been converted to Christianity is being beaten and thrown into prison with Silas. They are singing praises to God. An earthquake happens and all the prisoners are set free, doors flinging wide open. The prison keeper is just about to take his own life, when Paul encourages him not to. He asks what he must do to be saved. He and his whole family come to know Christ as their Savior.

LESSON 95. HEAVEN
Revelation 21:2

ACTIVITY:
Make a crayon picture of heaven. Color your paper how you view heaven according to what you just heard. Make sure the crayon pictures you drew are colored in bright and vibrant colors, not light. Then when your picture is done, color over it with the yellow watercolor for the gold of heaven.

SUPPLIES:
- Crayons
- Paper
- Yellow water color paint or watered down yellow paint

DISCUSSION:
Heaven is going to be beautiful—make sure you know Jesus and I will see you there!

REVIEW VERSE:
Revelation 21:2

> 2 Then I, John,[a] saw the holy city, New Jerusalem, coming down out of heaven from God, prepared as a bride adorned for her husband

SUMMARY:
We cannot even imagine what heaven will be like, but we will be in God's presence which is the best. God does not force us to be with Him. He has made a way for us. We can receive or reject the free gift God has provided for us in Christ Jesus. Romans 10:9 says that "If you confess with your mouth the Lord Jesus and believe in your heart that God has raised Him from the dead, you will be saved." If God has shown you, that you need His forgiveness, you can pray this following prayer: "Lord, I know I am a sinner. I need you to wash me clean. Fill me with your Holy Spirit. Help me to live for you. Thank you for dying on the cross for my sins, so I could spend

eternity with you". If you are not connected to a Bible believing church, then I encourage you to do so. God loves you so much. If I don't meet you this side of eternity, I'll see you soon on the other side!

QUICK REFERENCE LESSON GUIDE

Please refer to the lesson numbers (not page numbers) below for these activities on various themes.

EDUCATION:
Math: 1, 36, 64, 70, 77, 88, 89
Science: 2, 4, 44, 46, 61, 62, 63, 64, 65, 66, 85, 90
P.E./Games: 3, 6, 17, 18, 38, 52, 53, 54, 56, 58, 64, 74, 78, 80, 92, 94
Acting: 8, 14, 21, 22, 23, 24, 25, 28, 29, 30, 35, 37, 43, 44, 61, 93, 94
Arts/Crafts: 1. 4, 10, 20, 32, 45, 47, 48, 49, 51, 71, 87, 90
Music: 23, 24, 33, 92

SEASONS AND HOLIDAYS:
Valentine's Day: 3, 20, 30, 38, 50, 57, 64, 71, 76, 78, 83, 91, 92
Easter: 84, 85, 86, 87, 88
4th of July: 6, 23, 24, 31, 37, 43, 60, 70
Summer/Outdoor Fun: 15, 18, 55, 63, 65, 68, 63
Harvest/Fall: 10, 14, 39, 40, 43, 59, 67, 77

FRUIT OF THE SPIRIT:

Love: 3, 20, 30, 38, 50, 57, 58, 64, 71, 76, 78, 80, 83, 87, 91
Joy: 20, 36, 77, 84, 90, 92, 94
Peace: 20, 26, 27, 28, 41, 72, 91, 95
Patience: 7, 13, 20, 50, 91
Kindness: 6, 9, 12, 14, 20, 21, 26, 27, 36, 39, 40, 92
Goodness: 9, 13, 20, 21, 23, 27, 36, 39, 40, 92
Faithfulness: 2, 10, 20, 24, 28, 29, 41, 42, 44, 45, 46, 50, 58, 63, 66, 81, 91
Gentleness: 5, 8, 20, 54, 69, 70, 84, 92
Self-Control: 13, 20, 25, 43, 52, 91

EXTRA ACTIVITIES

Desserts: 6, 9, 12, 13, 14, 26, 35, 36, 40, 43, 48, 67, 75, 76, 81, 88, 89, 90
Ministry: 11, 30, 38, 71, 78, 83

ABOUT THE AUTHOR

God has blessed me with the best family ever who has taken this up and thought you and your family might be encouraged by these activities as well. Thank you Mom and John, Derrick, and my wonderful husband Mark, and my favorites Preston, Atticus, Chanan and Elisabeth. Thank you Lea, Rachel and Josh. You all did a great job! I really appreciate everything. Mostly, thank you Jesus for dying on the cross for all my sins, and making a way for me to spend eternity with you. You are everything I could ever want or need.